Islamic Finance Practices

Velid Efendic
Editor

Islamic Finance Practices

Experiences from South Eastern Europe

palgrave
macmillan

Editor
Velid Efendic
University of Sarajevo
Sarajevo, Bosnia and Herzegovina

ISBN 978-3-030-34419-1 ISBN 978-3-030-34420-7 (eBook)
https://doi.org/10.1007/978-3-030-34420-7

This Palgrave Macmillan imprint is published by the registered company Springer Nature Switzerland AG
The registered company address is: Gewerbestrasse 11, 6330 Cham, Switzerland

Preface

Islamic banking and finance is a rapidly growing area in the last two decades spreading across the world in all continents. Its success has led to numerous new Islamic banks, Islamic windows, investments funds, Takaful companies and other financial institutions and products. Recently, Southeastern Europe (SEE) is also identified as a new market and new region with fast growing interest for Islamic finance. Although it is still in the early phase of its development in SEE, Islamic finance recording the rapid development in last decade has created a need for research on related topics, from the fundamental principles to the SCR, investment banking and finally, to Islamic banking. This book is the product of the Sarajevo Islamic and Finance conference held in June 2018 in Sarajevo organised by European Association for Islamic Economics, Banking and Finance, with partners School of Economics and Business and Universiti Utara Malaysia. This conference traditionally gathers Islamic banking, economics and finance academicians, experts and students all over the world who discuss a wide range of topics in this field. After rigorous selection phase and blind review process provided by Palgrave Macmillan, the final text of the book consists of the seven chapters where the original research results are presented. Authors of the selected chapters are the respected scholars and professionals who made an excellent work using the synergy of the knowledge/research skills of academicians and experiences of the professionals. As such, all topics consist of the theoretical as well as practical overview of the researched area. Finally, the selected chapters covered the seven research areas.

In the first chapter, authors covered the history of economic thought hidden within the archives of Abrahamic religions where we can find discussion of main topics related to the markets and ethic from the perspective of the Abrahamic religions with special reference to the Islamic economics. The authors concluded that: "the Islamic economics principles are mainly of an ethical nature, therefore, the thorough understanding of market norms will commission the ability to predict the correct usage of approved Islamic financial instruments by Islamic financial institutions and other players within the financial market".

The second chapter covers the topic of exploring the epistemology of utility function in Islamic economics. Here we have presented the concept of "utility" in Islamic economics and development. The special reference is given to the capacity development in Islamic economics where the "utility" is divided into two major forms that are holistic utility and atomistic utility. The authors concluded that "The development of society and markets, within an Islamic framework, should be conducted by the holy man and scholars; as they can directly influence the factors behind holistic utility".

Islamic approach to Corporate Social Responsibility (SCR) in scientific research with CSR overview in banking sector of Bosnia and Herzegovina is presented within the third chapter. Here we have discussion of the Islamic approach to CSR in the literature as well as the theoretical foundations of the CSR. In addition to this, authors provided a short overview of the CSR in Bosnia and Herzegovina in conventional as well as in Islamic banking. Finally, comprehensive overview and analysis of the available literature on CSR is provided as well. The conclusion is that "causes of insufficient research in this area on a global scale could be that Islamic financial institutions and Islamic Scholars are observing corporate social responsibility as a part of Sharia and not as a separate entity".

The special case of CSR in the Muslim tradition is endowments of properties, land and money known as waqf. In the fourth chapter, we have presented potentials of waqfs from a socio-economic perspective on the case of Bosnia and Herzegovina. Here we have presented a definition and main principles of waqf and endowments in Muslim societies. In addition to this, the short overview of the literature on waqf is provided as well and special reference is given to the analysis of the waqf potentials in Bosnia and Herzegovina. Empirical findings on the perception of waqf in

Bosnia and Herzegovina and the role of the Muslim community in creating awareness about waqf are given as well. The authors concluded that a lack of awareness of waqf principles influenced waqf development negatively. However, waqifs and the members of the Islamic community are still of great support for waqf and its role that it can play in increasing the social justice and development.

In the fifth chapter, authors talk on efficient diversification with Shariah-compliant stocks on the cases from the Southeast European capital markets. Starting from Markovich diversification, the comprehensive literature and theory overview with special emphasis to the Islamic finance is provided. The empirical research is conducted and original results are provided. Authors found that SEE region offers significant diversificationopportunities to the European investors. By spreading their stock market investments to SEE region, European investors could obtain better risk-return profiles.

Sixth chapter covers the credit risk assessment for an Islamic bank in Bosnia and Herzegovina. The authors provided an overview of the Basel rules and Advanced Internal Rating-Based (IRB) Approach. Through the adequate research methodology, empirical findings on the case of the Islamic bank from Bosnia and Herzegovina are provided as well. Finally, the conclusion of the authors is that "it became evident that financially troubled businesses have a lower level of liquidity ratios, higher leverage ratios, lower ratio of activity compared to financially healthy companies".

Finally, in the seventh chapter, authors presented the market rent value as a basis for profit margin calculation in home financings based on diminishing Musharakah with Ijarah on the case study from Bosnia and Herzegovina. Here we have presented an use of market rent for profit margin calculation. Finally, in the empirical results, we have presented the possibilities for implementation of the market rent-based profit margin model in Bosnia and Herzegovina. Authors concluded that "considering the trend of decreasing interest rates and profit margins for loans and an increase in market rents, accompanied by a decrease in interest rates and profit rates for deposits in BiH, it is expected that rent and interest rates/profit margins will get even closer to one another in the near future".

With all of the topics presented above, this book should be very useful source for future academics research in the field of Islamic finance as well as to the practitioners and potential investors in Islamic finance, especially in Southeastern Europe. As such, it should not be finished without a great support of many individuals and institutions to which we want to express our gratitude in this place as well. Also, we have to thank all of our partners, colleagues and volunteers who helped us to bring this book to the publication phase. I need to express my special gratitude to Mr. Anes Prentić who gave a very significant support to this project and without whose support, this project couldn't be finished in given time frame.

Finally, I would love to express our great honour and gratitude to our esteemed Professor Dr. Fikret Hadžić who was one of the organisers of the SIFEC conference and founders of the European Association for Islamic Economics, Banking and Finance. Professor Fikret Hadžić took active participation in the SIFEC 2018 as well; he has been present at the opening ceremony and gave a great support to this conference and whole project. Unfortunately, shortly after the conference happened, Professor Fikret Hadžić passed away and didn't get the opportunity to see this book published. Therefore, on behalf of all of the supporters of the Islamic finance in the world, I would love to use this opportunity to thank Professor Fikret Hadžić for all of his support and huge efforts he gave to the development of Islamic finance field in Bosnia and Herzegovina and abroad. This book is my/our "in memoriam" inheritance to the remembering of great man, professor, colleague, friend, husband and father. May God have mercy on his soul....

Sarajevo, Bosnia and Herzegovina
2019

Prof. Dr. Velid Efendic

Contents

List of Contributors

Almira Arnaut-Berilo School of Economics and Business, University of Sarajevo, Sarajevo, Bosnia and Herzegovina

Alija Avdukić Edinburgh Napier University, Edinburgh, UK;
Al-Maktoum College of Higher Education, Dundee, UK

Mensud Bisić School of Economics and Business, University of Sarajevo, Sarajevo, Bosnia and Herzegovina

Velid Efendic School of Economics and Business, University of Sarajevo, Sarajevo, Bosnia and Herzegovina

Fikret Hadžić School of Economics and Business in Sarajevo, University of Sarajevo, Sarajevo, Bosnia and Herzegovina

Aida Hanić Institute of Economic Sciences, Belgrade, Serbia

Migdat Hodžić International University of Sarajevo, Sarajevo, Bosnia and Herzegovina

Fawad Khaleel Al-Maktoum College of Higher Education, Dundee, UK;
Edinburgh Napier University, Edinburgh, UK

Anisa Lojo-Bajrić Bosna Bank International Sarajevo, Sarajevo, Bosnia and Herzegovina

Azra Osmanbegović ASA Banka, Sarajevo, Bosnia and Herzegovina

Nerma Saračević University of J.J. Strossmayer, Osijek, Croatia

Azra Zaimović School of Economics and Business, University of Sarajevo, Sarajevo, Bosnia and Herzegovina

List of Figures

Chapter 5

List of Tables

Chapter 5

Chapter 6

Chapter 7

CHAPTER 1

History of Economic Thought Hidden Within the Archives of Abrahamic Religions

Fawad Khaleel and Alija Avdukić

Key Topics

- Abrahamic Faiths
- Morality and Market Regulations

1 Introduction

The set of epistemological transformations which revolutionised the methodology of investigation by introducing empiricism marks the era of scientific revolution (Hooker, 4 August 2009). This methodology led to the construction of new ideas and theories inevitably contradicting and refuting previous doctrines through the manifestation of empirical evidence. The scientific revolution led to the 'Age of Enlightenment', which

F. Khaleel (✉) · A. Avdukić
Edinburgh Napier University, Edinburgh, UK
e-mail: F.Khaleel@napier.ac.uk

V. Efendic (ed.), *Islamic Finance Practices*,
https://doi.org/10.1007/978-3-030-34420-7_1

is also known as 'Age of Reasoning' with its strong focus on critical thinking and reasoning based on evidence rather than relying on the transcendental justifications of religion (Hackett, 4 August 2009). The English, German and French philosophers and intellectuals showed a very sceptical and captious approach towards religion. Furthermore, the French Encyclopaedism resulted in an understanding of religion as: 'an eternal hindrance to intellectual progress and … incapable of founding a genuine morality and a just social and political order' (Cassirer 1979: 136). This apparently detached religious ideology from social and economic spheres of life. It also diminished the impact of religious scripture, along with works of Aristotle, away from the locus of intellect and rationalism. This epoch also affected the nineteenth and twentieth centuries, when seen through the lens of philosophical positions adopted by many scholars. The practice of separating religion from the public sphere is elaborated by Nietzsche as cited in Schacht (1985: 443):

> 'The whole of European morality' is a part of 'what must now collapse' … 'When one gives up the Christian faith [or any other religion], one pulls the rights to Christian [or respective religion's] morality out under one's feet,' … it stands and falls with faith in God.' … The very conditional character of its [Religious value judgement's] right to existence is no longer felt,' and its …now reflected in people's 'intuitions' of 'what is good and evil'. Fundamentally it has the status of 'a command,' which 'has truth only if God is the truth'.

A religion's morality and its interpretation of 'good and evil' cannot act as a benchmark for a society, until the respective religion is perceived to be both divine and the most suitable direction towards securing a normative society. With the separation of religion in this epoch, morality and ethical guidance derived from religious teachings were also rejected by society. The licitness to authority was inherited by reason from the religion, and religious morality was replaced by 'methodological naturalism'. Kurtz defines methodological naturalism as a procedure for explaining natural phenomena concerning natural causes through the testing of hypotheses (as cited in Forrest 2000: 8). Religious ideology, on the other hand, was replaced by 'philosophical naturalism', which emphasised that 'nature is best accounted for by reference to material principles' rather than pneumatological explanations (Forrest 2000: 8). Galileo further elaborated this philosophy by explaining that 'nature never violates the terms of the laws imposed upon her' (numbers as cited in Lindberg and Numbers 2003: 267).

The approach detailed above resulted in bringing out more defined and structured market concepts and revolutionary methods of regulation and control, coinciding with the epistemological transformation of society. The Age of Enlightenment further proved to be the breeding ground for the progression of many disciplines, including the study of economics. It further opened the doors for the development of political and economic liberalism and prepared the foundations for modern secularism. The further technological and scientific advancements of civilisation during the following centuries, resulted in a general conclusion that from a psychological perspective, an individual with some education, better social integration and more fulfilled basic needs becomes less dependent on religious ideologies for psychological satisfaction and, thus, becomes less religious. In other words, the more an individual understands science the more critical he or she becomes towards religious doctrines. The future of religion, from a sociological perspective, is elaborated by Lenski (Lannaccone 1998: 1468):

> Sociology was thus from its inception ... committed to the positivist view that religion in the modern world is merely a survival from man's primitive past, and doomed to disappear in an era of science and general enlightenment.

Similarly, reflected by Freud's argument citing the exigency of eradicating religion from a cultural perspective, it is the proposed benefits projected by religion which can only be accomplished through scientific methods alleviating civilisation from strict religious regulations (Runzo 2001: 168). This meant that rigorous religious regulations can be replaced by an agile and efficient methodology based on scientific understanding, removing and superseding religion. Despite centuries of scientific development, media and information saturation combined with globalisation, religion still holds an incessant significance in today's world (Lannaccone 1998: 1468). Although there are many constraints on analysing the authenticity of real data regarding religion, however, most of the world's leading religions claim a healthy growth rate (The List: The World's Fastest Growing Religions, 14 August 2009). A steep increase in the membership growth of churches in the USA since the American revolution from 16 to about 60% of the population's attendance, and statistical data from the US Bureau of Labor suggests that the fraction of the population employed as clergy has remained constant during the last one and half centuries (Lannaccone 1998: 1469).

Religious surveys suggest that religious beliefs are not inversely proportionate to rises in income or an increase in educational levels (Lannaccone 1998: 1468). The methodology which allowed civilisation to interpret natural phenomena into scientific facts has also allowed the cultivation of a better understanding towards religious ideologies, and hence, a new religious contextualization accompanying postmodernism has emerged. In this process of recontextualization, the church shifted from its position of an absolute ban on interest to a position which permits this practice. Accordingly, the church's understanding of contemporary concepts of interest is not of the same nature when compared to previously held views (Munby 1956). This position is contrary to historical approaches, where divine religious texts were contextualised to reflect the environment in which they were expressed or revealed.

Moreover, the challenges faced by religions in the postmodernism era have instigated a recontextualization of religious ideologies to find solutions for today's problems. This process has increasingly brought religion into the limelight. During the last decades, political conflicts based on religion, religious-based economic reforms have ensued, alongside the influence of religion on culture, media, technology, medical science and the demand for food and beverage. The cartoons of Prophet Muhammad (pbuh) published by Danish newspaper, Jyllands-Posten, during 2005, are illustrative examples of developments in local disputes on religion's impact and comprehension, replicating patterns of global conflicts (Wæver, 18 August 2009).

The increase in religious involvement in the operations of society, especially, within the market highlights further challenges for regulatory authorities. This has led to changes in the regulatory approaches utilised by many authorities, to accommodate religiously led market operations. The UK's Financial Services Authority introduced significant measures between the enactment of the Finance Act 2000 to the introduction of the Finance Act 2007, to accommodate Islamic financial products within a British market (Ainley et al. 2007: 8), while France, in spite of its historical roots concerning religious scepticism, adjusted its legal and taxation system through legislative reforms, to introduce Islamic financial products (Legal Week, 20 August 2009). Such reformations are driven by many factors, including the search for sources of liquidity for the economy rather than pragmatic factors (Legal Week, 20 August 2009). In the current era, state and society's receptivity towards religion has oscillated between complete scepticism to a progressive stance. While in a progressive mode state and society accept and encourage religious economic practice within a controlled environment, if religious economic practices result in tangible or intangible benefits. This has opened a door of opportunity for religious ideologues to promote the acceptability of religion in post-postmodernism and reinvigorate the perception of outcomes, from a religiously motivated economic and social activity. However, religious ideologies will need to deconstruct historical attempts to regulate the market using religious principles. This process of deconstruction could highlight the misconstruction of the implementation of religious principles.

2 Market Regulations and Ethics: Religiously Informed Regulative Environment

Trade through wilful means of exchange largely appears in all recorded human history. The need and necessity of trade materialised in the creation of markets somewhere in between 12,000 and 10,000 BC, whereas a well-structured and moderately defined working model of a market system can be seen as far back as 6000 BC, in the form of bartering in Mesopotamia (Ryan, 23 March 2009). Until the early epoch between 3000 BC and 500 BC, market mechanisms were moderately easy in processes and methods of functioning without having introduced complicated and complex definitions, and deceptions. With the passage of time the complexity speared into the market, it also brought with it factors like fraud, deception, exploitation and dishonesty. To mitigate unhealthy market elements, the practice of regulations was introduced which supervised and govern the ethics in the functions of markets. These regulations were derived and extracted from the social ethics and morals which prevailed within society. The derived values of social ethics and morals were constructed on the general perception of definition of good and bad perceived within the culture and religion. Without a formal regulatory institution, markets were regulated through implementing the practices that were created by the social dimensions of culture and religion.

3 Judaism, It's Effects and Influence on Market Regulations

Judaism as an ancient religion discusses market regulation in Judaic law, known as *Halakhah. Halakhah* is categorised by two dimensions: one explains normative standards mainly based on rights, status and responsibility, while the other dimension explicates the collection of solutions permitted, when dealing with economic and social problems (Resnicoff as cited in Lange and Kandel 2005: 363). The main primary sources of *Halakhah* are the Torah, Mishnah and Talmud. Moses had two kinds of revelations from the God: one comprises five books called the 'written law' or the 'written Torah', while the second body of revelations were oral traditions transmitted from one generation to another (Resnicoff as cited in Lange and Kandel 2005: 364). Oral traditions were later recorded and compiled in 188CE under the name of Mishnah, Thereafter, during the historical period of Gemara (500CE), scholars discussed and debated on the Mishnah and the 'written Torah' (Leiter, 2 September 2009). The collection of these debates was compiled together and named Talmud in 350CE, while another collection called Babylonian Talmud was later compiled in 500CE. Rabbis employed the streams of interpretation from these sources to develop an entire legal system. The rich text surrounding the *Halakhah* and the methodology used by rabbis in the past make it complicated to draw a clear line between the primary sources and secondary sources within the body of literature.

The *Nezikin*, the fourth order of Mishnah, specifies the laws of tort along with civil and criminal law while in the main primary sources, the wisdom for market regulations is scattered. The Talmud discusses legal issues along with non-legal subjects; therefore, the rabbis have devised a system of 'authoritative legal codes' which only focuses on the legal issues and is arranged in sequence of subjects (Leiter, 2 September 2009). In 'legal codes', Maimonide's Mishneh Torah is considered as one of the major collections and is placed among the primary sources of law (Leiter, 2 September 2009). Rabbi Karo further discussed the Maimonide's work and created a simplified form of legal codes under the name of *Shulchan Aruch* (Friedman 2001). The main concentrates of Maimonide's, Mishneh Torah, focus on market regulation which can be narrowed down to: book eleven of Mishnah Torah, *Sefer Nezikin* (Book of Damages) which elaborates on the laws of theft and damage; the book twelve: *Sefer Kinyan* (Book of Acquisition) lays out the laws of sales, entitlements, law of agency and partnership; and book thirteen: *Sefer Mishpatim* (Book of Civil Laws) addresses laws of leasing and hiring, laws of borrowing and bailment, laws of creditors and debtors, and the laws of plaintiffs and defendants. Book fourteen: *Sefer Shoftim* (Book of Judges) discusses the laws of evidence and jurisprudence (Leiter, 2 September 2009). According to the *Anshei Knesset HaGedolah* (The Men of the Great Synagogue), the Torah is composed of laws which are classified into three categories (Maharal, 23 January 2010). The first category called *Mishpatim* contains a kind of positive law that can be comprehended and constructed by humans; *mitzvoth* consists of laws which can be explained by logic and applies the use of rationale; however, construction of these laws is beyond human capability and, hence, requires divine revelation (Maharal, 23 January 2010). The third category is called *chukim* which contains divine laws which cannot be rationalised by human beings (Maharal, 23 January 2010). Most regulatory market laws fall within the parameters of *mitzvoth* and *mishpatim*.

The *Halakhah* insists individuals are to strive, to be ethical and abide by the normative aspects of law by exceeding more than the legal requirements. This is derived from the verses (Deuteronomy 6:18): 'You shall do that which is fair and good in the sight of the Lord' (Friedman 2001: 77). The Talmudic sages devised an ethical hierarchy, to measure the ethics of people. The peak of this hierarchy was the 'way of the pious' while the lowest was 'the wicked person' (Friedman 2001). This system measured the length by which an individual in relation to Judaic ethics exceeded or fell-short of the legal requirements. Although not much is known about the effects of the system, when considering religious and social taboos of the society, it can be argued that this system could have motivated and recognised individuals performing ethically in the market and society. This system also discouraged the practice of swindling, allowing the law to serve its profound purpose. This also served as a benchmark for fair competition within the market, although the annotation for the concept of ethics and fair competition was based on the teachings of primary sources. One understanding of anticompetitive practices in the market was to open a store selling the identical commodity to the adjacent store (Friedman 2001). The emphasis on market honesty in the scriptures led to the development of concepts of consumer protection that would help in mitigating market exploitation like rigorous labour, fraudulent activities, deceptive advertising, deceptive packaging and deception in quality, as violations of *Halakhah* principles (Friedman 2001). Many of other ethical dimensions introduced into the market were concepts of 'just weight', transparency and fair judgement. Talmud (T. Bava Bathra 88a) also instructed the weights to be cleaned weekly and scales to be dredged after every transaction, for putting into practice the concept of just weight (Friedman 2001). Furthermore, the Torah's statement (Leviticus 25:14): 'If you sell something to your neighbour or buy something from your neighbour's hand, you shall not wrong one another' was interpreted by the Talmud (T. Bava Metzia 50b) into the concept of fair price (Friedman 2001). Further, the law of *hona'ah* (swindling) was introduced, as assumed by historians it had two-dimensional effects. First, it fixed the profit margin to 16%. The second dimension was the mechanism for price-fixing which was also based on this concept, that is '[basic purchase price + marketing expenses] + one sixth of purchase = fair selling price'. The 'basic purchase price' included the expense and overheads of the seller, and one-sixth of the 'basic purchase price' was added as the profit margin to what it is to be a 'fair selling price' of that product. The law of *hona'ah* when applied to the price-fixing meant that the price of a product will increase by one-sixth, every time it is sold and bought. Any selling price above or below the fair price was considered *hona'ah* while hoarding and any other mechanism for raising fair prices were also prohibited. Other than this, the prices of necessities and drugs were sometimes fixed using many different methods (Baron 1952: 255).

Historical accounts suggest that the approach of price-fixings was neither effective nor efficient economically or socially, when compared to the price ceiling implemented by Diocletian (Baron 1952: 255). Although it could be argued that Diocletian had help in implementing it effectively through a vast workforce, in terms of his army and an extensive number of officials, which the rabbis lacked. The rabbi's approach to any economic problem was through the ordinance of psychological and ethical solutions which sometimes were impractical and resulted in financial losses (Baron 1952: 255). By devising the practical methods to ensure the practice of fair prices, rabbis formulated very strict and unsustainable market regulations. Furthermore, to tackle the problem of ever-changing market conditions and shifting market functions rabbis created a system of exception regulations which led to a further generation of exemptions from exception regulations (Baron 1952: 255). This added to the complexity in market regulations and created an arduous task of market monitoring. The function of market monitoring was supported from the Torah's account of Tabernacle (Exodus 38:21):

> Moses wanted to make it evident that he and the builders of the Tabernacle did not divert any of the precious metals for their own personal use and he therefore used others to audit the records.

The arduous task of monitoring the market was assigned by *exilarch* to the Rab's (sages), who were appointed as 'market supervisors' (Hezser 1993: 172). The office of market supervisor started surveillance of the market for the correct practice of 'just weight' while later the authority of fixing and controlling the prices was also added to its responsibilities (Neusner 1972: 112). Historical sources do expand on the civil implications of the governing laws, although accounts which could collaborate the efficiency, effectiveness and detail methods of the functionality of the office are sparse. However, it could be argued that the lack of data suggests that there may not be any major concerns at any level regarding the effectiveness of market supervisors; otherwise, it would have been criticised as a model unfit for market regulation and, hence, would have been documented. The present form of market supervisors among rabbis can be witnessed in the form of Kosher Inspectors appointed by different Jewish congregations.

The system under *Halakhah* governance undermines its subjects to be mindful of their daily social activities that can affect and influence the environment and society. Judaism also shows a very positive attitude towards social and economic well-being. Primary sources claim wealth and peace to be rewards from God. The Talmud (T. Bava Metzia 42a) also advises that one should keep a third of their wealth invested in business, one-third invested in land (housing market) and the remaining third in a liquid form (Friedman 2001). Diversifying the investments of assets is considered as a protection from imperilment of poverty by reducing the overall risk.

4 The Ethical Code of Christianity and Its Paternal Approach on Market Regulations

In the era of ancient Romans, 80% of the population consisted of slaves (Hunt 1981: 2). At the time, the Empire had few treatises, which acted as guidelines on supervision, control and punishment of slaves by the slave masters (Hunt 1981: 2). The collapse of the Roman Empire resulted in a system of feudal hierarchy, later to be known as feudalism. The white feather of this era was the society's acknowledgement of mutual obligation, which was pre-decided through the social hierarchy (Hunt 1981: 2). The system of dispute resolution was operated through the social ladder based on the obligations of social classes and customs of the time. The lord of the manor used to judge on the disputes among serfs while the disputes between serf and lords were taken to the court of overlord, who used to act as a vassal to the lord (Hunt 1981: 2). The overlord had the power to impose sanctions on the lord, while each dispute was judged independently according to the customs and traditions. The enforcement of sanctions was enacted through the long hierarchy of vassals based on social status. This gave the society an infrastructure to regulate itself.

The infrastructure alone could not ensure the smooth running of everyday transactions in the society and could not justify the feudal status quo. For this purpose, feudal lords, secular or religious required an ideology that is '[a set of] ideas and belief that tend to justify morally a society's social and economic relationships' (Hunt 1981: 2). By this time, Christian values and traditions were embedded into public and private life; therefore, feudalism took on board the moral codes of the Judeo-Christian traditions referred to as Christian corporate ethics (Hunt 1981: 4).

Christian scholars suggest that their faith does not provide a simple model for society to follow; instead, it states the limits of social relations within which Christians are supposed to act (Munby 1956: 25). For markets, there again are no direct laws and legislators mainly concentrate of laws directed towards individual's application of capital in the market (Donald 1989: 114).

Christian corporate ethic has roots in both the Old and New Testaments, strongly focusing on poverty alleviation and prevention. This resulted in Christian corporate ethic's main emphasis centred on the concept of obligation of the wealthy towards the poor (Hunt 1981: 7). Compared to Judaism's positive approach, Christianity demonstrates a somewhat negative attitude towards economic gains, as Matthew (19:23–24), Mark (10:24–25) and Luke (18:24–25) all refer to this philosophy as: 'It is easier for a camel to go through the eye of a needle than for a rich man to enter the kingdom of God'. Hunt while discussing the Gospel of Luke elaborates that Christianity: 'Condemned the rich simply because they were rich and praised the poor because they were poor' (1981: 7).

Theologians, such as Clement of Alexandria, developed this approach in a practical application by conceptualising people with wealth, as people entrusted by God to administer wealth on behalf of the poor. This concept assigned the responsibility of social welfare to the wealthy. Historically, it is argued that the practicality of Christian corporate ethics was mainly developed by the work of many scholars, including the History of Economic Thought (21 July 2009):

> St. Thomas and the Dominicans, who dug out of Aristotle and the Bible the necessary arguments ... [such as the] private property was a "conventional" human arrangement with no moral implications, and furthermore, it had the nice side-effect of stimulating economic activity and thus general welfare.

The philosophical religious position regarding wealth plays an important role determining how the market is regulated, especially for Christianity where the definition of right and wrong in the economic sphere is considered to be same as in the social sphere (Hunt 1981: 9). At the time, this meant that every transaction should be conducted according to the social, traditional ethics and principles prevailing in society. This principle was chosen as the methodology for regulating the market. It laid down the level of care to be shown to the customers, competitors, producers and prescribed the humane treatment of debtors. Furthermore, this also allowed society to practice and judge the legitimacy of the market place, by applying definitions of good and bad which prevailed in the social sphere.

The Thomists furthermore constituted the application of commutative justice of Aristotle with the Bible. The notion of Aristotle that 'just exchange ratio of goods ... should be in proportion to their "intrinsic worth" to men' was introduced into market regulations (the History of Economic Thoughts, 21 July 2009). Aristotle also argued that individuals have different needs to each other, which meant the intrinsic worth (*bonitas intrinseca*) of goods would be different (the History of Economic Thoughts, 21 July 2009). This concept was combined with the biblical rule: 'Do unto others as you would have them do unto you', and the concept of Just Price (*justum pretium*) was introduced. The idea of Just Price was further anatomised in Christian corporate ethics as (Hunt 1981: 9):

> one that compensate the seller for his efforts in transporting the good and in finding the buyer at a rate that was just sufficient to maintain the seller at his customary or traditional station in life.

It was a moral duty of every player within the market to buy and sell at a Just Price. This concept was also introduced to discourage profit maximisation through exploitation and profit generation for the sole purpose of accumulating wealth, which according to the traditions of the time was considered immoral. The teachings of the Christian corporate code portrayed to society that the pareto optimal exchange of good or services is only possible at the Just Price. This meant that any gain above the Just Price would make someone worst off. Due to this understanding, the Italian Dominican theologian, St. Thomas Aquinas, denounced the motivation for profit (Huberman 1937: 9). Aquinas further suggested the relationship of labour and cost in calculating the Just Price, while St Augustine's edict named want as a measure of Just Price whereas, on the other hand, St Bernardino and St Antonino argued the scarcity of goods was directly correlated to its Just Price (Grice-Hutchison 1978: 85). Later, the School of Salamanca's research on Aquinas' notion of Just Price further contributed to the theory of value.

Around the fifteenth century, there was a consensus among scholars that the Just Price depends on scarcity and on the kind of need it fulfils. Francisco de Vitoria further elaborated this concept by dividing the goods into two categories: the goods whose price is fixed by the state and the goods whose price is not fixed (Grice-Hutchison 1978: 85). He further presents two concepts that is: the Just Price and the Fancy Price: the Just Price for items of basic need is based on the market price without consideration for costs of production, while the Fancy Price is the price of luxurious goods (Grice-Hutchison 1978: 99). Saravia de la Calle also follows Aristotle's lead and discards the cost of production as a determining factor arguing that Just Price depends on following three things: scarcity of goods, money and merchants (Grice-Hutchison 1978: 99). He further epitomises that (Grice-Hutchison 1978: 100):

> Those who measure the just price by the labour, costs and risk… are greatly in error, and still more so are those who allow a certain profit of a fifth or a tenth. For the just price arises from abundance or scarcity of goods, merchants, and money, as has been said, and not from costs, labour, and risk. If we had to consider labour and risk in order to assess the just price,

> no merchant would suffer loss, nor would abundance or scarcity of goods and money enter into question.

Covarrubias also acknowledged Saravia's approach, while Juan de Salas in 1617 added utility as another factor to Saravia's concept of Just Price (Grice-Hutchison 1978: 100).

The Christian corporate code also discourages the concept of business opportunity, while a moral sealing was placed on profit generation, which allowed the seller to generate only the profit required for the fulfilment of his or her basic needs. These concepts were embedded into the market by the church, and it derived these laws from verses of the bible.

Another important code of Christian corporate ethics was the limitation on possession of such tools or assets as a levy for satisfying a debt, which provided a means of earning to a debtor (Hunt 1981: 6). Old Testament verses contain such examples: 'No Man shall take the nether or the upper millstone to pledge: for he taketh a man's life to pledge'[1] which abstract this principle of debt collection (Hunt 1981: 6).

Church derivation of market laws resulted in an absolute prohibition on interest by the 12th Canon of the First Council of Carthage (345) and 36th Canon of the Council of Aix (789) (Catholic Encyclopedia, 28 April 2009). Aristotle's stance on usury and Thomas Aquinas' understanding that money has no intrinsic worth, combined with the biblical rule of 'earning without labour' resulted in interpretation of the biblical verses: 'Upon a stranger thou mayest lend upon usury, but unto thy brother thou shalt not lend upon usury' (Deuteronomy 23:20), into an absolute prohibition of interest (the History of Economic Thoughts, 21 July 2009). This later resulted in a bill being passed by the government of England which prohibited usury. The bill stated that (Huberman 1937: 39):

> For any manner of usury, increase, lucre, gain or interest to be had, received or hoped for, over and above the sum or sums so lent…upon pain of forfeiture… of the sum or sums so lent…as also of the usury… and also upon pain or imprisonment.

St. Thomas, Lessius, de Lugo, Luther, Zwingli and several other theologians and Canonists of the Middle Ages agreed to this position (Catholic

[1] Deut 24:6.

Encyclopedia, 28 April 2009). To emphasis the gravity of the law which prohibited interest, the Council of Vienne (1311) declared that any one maintaining the view that charging of interest is legal, she/he would be punished as a heretic (Catholic Encyclopedia, 28 April 2009). This emphasis shows that the focus on economic issues was as strong as that placed on social problems. Despite the strong belief in the pre-eminence of these principles, laws derived from them were violated (Hunt 1981: 39). One of the many reasons for this violation was the absence of a system which could proactively countercheck the violation. The ratio between practice and violation of these laws is not clear; however, in general terms it is accepted that these laws, in one form or another, regulated the market and every transaction within the market was judged independently in the light of these laws.

The church used to be a momentous and dominant actor within society and people of the age were mainly influenced by the concept of sin. This factor also supported the sustainable implementation of these laws within the market. A shift in the Christian position concerning interest started when the Protestant theologian, John Calvin, argued for allowing interest to be charged upon the rich (Catholic Encyclopedia, 28 April 2009). This argument was later transformed into a coded system by one of Calvin's disciple, which was followed by the lenitive approach of Catholic scholars towards this issue (Catholic Encyclopedia, 28 April 2009). At the time of Pope Benedict XIV, Scipio Maffei in his treaties, argued for similar positioning in Catholicism (Catholic Encyclopedia, 28 April 2009). This shift in theological positioning on the legitimacy of interest baring loans was largely welcomed by the economists of the time, as major civil laws were aligned with Canon Law. This development was superseded by the abolishment of civil laws prohibiting the charge of interest by states across Europe. Currently, the Holy See condemns the 'exacting of anything over and above capital, except when, by reason of some special circumstance … called *extrinsic titles*' (Catholic Encyclopedia, 28 April 2009). It also asserts the charging of *usury* (high interest rates) as injustice; however, he attests to the legitimacy of current practice of interest in the financial industry and permits it (Catholic Encyclopedia, 28 April 2009). Holy See also considers loans for ecclesiastical purposes as judicially just (Catholic Encyclopedia, 28 April 2009).

Theologically, it is argued that there is no absolute prohibition on interest detailed in the Old Testament and the only references available found in Exodus (22:25) and Deuteronomy (23:19–20) proscribe the charging of interest within the Jewish community from Jewish lenders, while the New Testament does not divulgate any clear ruling on this matter (Catholic Encyclopedia, 28 April 2009). Verses in St. Luke (vi, 34, 35) are taken by some theologians as an indirect denouncement against charging interest, while others argue against this by using the Patristic traditions which prohibit the universal application of such verses (Catholic Encyclopedia, 28 April 2009). Theologians have also highlighted that laws prohibiting interest were mainly derived using ethical grounds. The absence of these ethical grounds regarding the manner in which modern financial operations are conducted due to the framework of regulatory constraints has resulted in the abolishment of prohibition of interest within Canon Law (Catholic Encyclopedia, 28 April 2009). Overall, in this process of evolution, from the time the Canon Law attended to civil law as a chaperone, to the point where civil law oversees Canon Law, there has been repositioning of market regulations in Christianity. Although there are many social, theological and philosophical reasons for this repositioning, however, one of them is also the development in market and trade.

From the period of twelfth to fifteenth century, the long-distance trade revived the local weekly markets into large scale market fairs. This change further effected the efficient implementation of market laws. The merchants emerged as the key market players for the capital flow of the lords. The lord of the province levied taxes and in return offered security during the fair and made special arrangements for the secure travel of merchants to and from the fair (Huberman 1937: 24). The merchants sought to reduce the risk of loss through robbery during travel and devised a mechanism to penalise feudal lords for any negligence in the administration of their safe passage to and from the fairs. In these circumstances, all the merchants derived from areas infamous for and sensitive to robbery were banned from participation in any of the fairs (Huberman 1937: 24). This could severely paralyse the business activities of that province, which would result in material loss for the lord of the province. The fairs were not only vital for trading but also because of its financial activities. Major activities involved money changing transactions. The liquidity of capital in money exchanging business also led to processing of loans, debt negotiation and letters of credit (Huberman 1937: 24). During the fifteenth century, the active business markets resulted in the development of commercial cities which had year-round markets (Hunt 1981: 15). This was the start of an end to feudal methodology, which was mainly based on the ownership of soil. The feudal lords had very little knowledge of new trade techniques in the market, while the lack of further advancements in the Christian corporate code resulted in markets being administrated in an identical fashion to the manorial estates, that is the feudal lords used to impose taxes, collect dues, exercise monopoly and run the court of law, as they would do on manors (Huberman 1937: 29). The market was by far very different to the manorial estates and the practice of administrating markets similarly to manorial estates, led to a very rigid system of market regulations. From the merchants' point of view, the lack of flexibility in the system meant that it could no longer administer trade activity in the market, and, thus, resulting in the collapse of the feudal system.

5 Conclusion

Islam proclaims to be the last in a series of revealed monotheistic religions acknowledging the existence of certain analogous features with Judaism and Christianity. Islam shares many identical similarities with Judaism regarding the pattern and structure of order in its literary sources. The traditions of Prophet Muhammad called *al-ḥadīth* and the revealed scripture, *Qur'ān*, are the two primary sources in Islam. *Sharīah* (Islamic Law) signifies the divine system which consists of a set of rules and regulations derived mainly from primary sources. While *fiqh* is an (Calder(a), 6 August 2010):

> academic discipline whereby scholars described and explored the Sharīa [.It] designates a human activity and cannot be ascribed to God or (usually) the Prophet.

In the process of derivation of law within *fiqh*, the sources of law are deduced, and the methodology is extrapolated by the *uṣūl al-fiqh* (principles of jurisprudence), while the works of *furū*ᶜ delineate the norms of the law (Calder(b), 6 August 2010). Islamic finance which is supposedly based on the Islamic economics principles is primarily the biggest project of re-implementation of religious regulations on the market. The modern financial system and current economic understandings are reasonably uncharted territories for Islamic law. The jurist's tool of *fatwā* (legal opinion) and innovative financial engineering is being collectively used to reconcile the difference between the Islamic economic principles and current financial mechanisms. In this process of reconciliation, there is a continual shift in legal positioning within Islamic law. This shift in legal positioning will further increase as the jurists develop a better understanding of financial world and as the demand for sophisticated financial instruments increases. The shift in legal positioning can produce positive and negative effects on the fundamentals of Islamic Sciences and thought. To increase the probability of a positive effect, it is vital for Islamic legal practitioners to be aware of similar historical archetypes.

In Christianity's endeavour to regulate the market, the regulations were designed to consuetude individuals to use social norms within the market rather than market norms. Although it is possible to stimulate the practice of social norms within market, however, it is a strenuous task to achieve this, only by plain and direct regulations.[2] Therefore, it is important for the development of Islamic law within Islamic finance, to distinguish and comprehend the market and social norms for authentic implementation of Islamic legal axioms such as 'commanding good and forbidding evil'. Moreover, the Islamic economics principles are mainly of an ethical nature; therefore, the thorough understanding of market norms will commission the ability to predict the correct usage of approved Islamic financial instruments by Islamic financial institutions and other players within the financial market. This ability will further help in translating the ethical dimension of Islamic economic principles into Islamic financial instruments.

Judaic methodology of regulating the market is similar to Islam's, as both faiths provide basic transcendental principles aimed at attaining a level of morality within the market. These principles, such as the principle of *lifnei iver* (misleading) extracted from *Leviticus* (19:14), the principle of *geneivat da'at*, dealing with the prohibition of deception in the market, laws of conflicts of interest[3] and many more, form the backbone of Jewish regulations in the market. Friedman, L. W. and Friedman, H. H., have rigorously argued for the possibility of preventing the 2008 financial meltdown, if these principles were adopted and introduced within the market (12 August 2010). However, the previous attempt by Judaism to

[2] For further reading consult, Dan Ariely's work 'Predictable Irrationality'.

[3] For further reading consult: Klainman, R. (2000). 'Conflicts of Interest of Public Officials in Jewish law—Prohibitions, Scope, and Limitations'. In H. G. Sprecher, ed., *Jewish Law Association Studies X: The Jerusalem 1998 Conference Volume*, pp. 93–116, Binghamton NY: Global Publications of SUNY at Binghamton.

regulate the market resulted in a formulation of very strict and unsustainable market regulations by rabbis. Furthermore, the ever-changing market conditions and shifting market functions of the time resulted in the creation of a system of exception regulations which led to a further generation of exemptions from exception regulations, leading to a complex structure of market regulations and an arduous task of implementing and practising them (Baron 1952: 255).

The prescribed principles within Islam may add the much-needed morality within the financial world. However, the current framework of individual *Sharīah* boards in Islamic financial institutions around the world has resulted in different, versatile and contradictory addition of rulings within *Sharīah* law. In future, the global reconciliation of these rules could lead to a structure to exemption regulations, especially when tools like *istihsan* are utilised. Therefore, there is a need to re-evaluate the methodological structure currently used to implement the market regulations of *Sharīah*, in the operations of financial institutions. The classification of ethical actions in *Halakhah*, designed to encourage people, to be on the ethical and the normative side of the law by exceeding more than the legal requirements, could also act as an exemplar for *Sharīah* scholars in Islamic finance. Such a classification of Islamic financial instruments could stimulate more ethically based financial solutions. It may not only provide more options suited to spiritual preferences of individuals, but it may also increase awareness of Islamic finance along with satisfying concerns of those critical of it.

One of the major shifts in Christianity's approach towards market regulations was the evolution in understanding of interest. The comprehension of interest as injustice towards the borrower was later transformed into the understanding that the lack of interest is unjust to lender. There was also a massive shift within *Sharīah* law, during the development of Islamic finance. This shift provided an allowance for investment, into the companies with an income of 5% or less from prohibited sources (like *riba*). Although, within this concept, the Islamic financial institutions are still not allowed to benefit from return on investment, from the specific income gained from means considered illegitimate within *Sharīah*, by the firm in which the capital was invested. However, this does indicate a change in position as the classical jurists, would have hampered such an involvement of income from prohibited means. Compared to Christianity, Islam has the prohibition of interest, subscribed in its primary sources; therefore, such a shift could present significant challenges for the future jurists, as the current position of 5% leeway, in future could lead to an increase in this percentage allowance.

The historical attempts at regulating the market with religiously based regulations have either resulted in rigid and strict regulations or chimerical regulations which could neither be implemented nor practised efficiently. Few of the causes for such regulations are the inadequate understanding of economics, incomplete comprehension on economic effects of newly formulated laws and inept knowledge of market mechanisms, within the scholarship of religious institutions. *S͟harīah* scholars within Islamic finance currently also face a similar dilemma. The current trend in the market is to promote *S͟harīah* scholars possessing an understanding of finance; however, the drawback to such a solution is the improbability of having professionals with expertise in both fields, due to the depth of knowledge required in economics and finance, and the level of acquaintance, required in *S͟harīah* to produce comprehensive *S͟harīah* compliant financial solutions. The possible solutions to these and above-listed problems could be the re-establishment of the institution of ***hisb'a*** on a global scale. Historically, this institution not only regulated the market but also scholars. If such an institution is re-established, it would not only reconcile the different opinions of scholars but also provide a joint platform for *S͟harīah* scholars, economists and financial analysts, so that the real effects of proposed *S͟harīah* compliant solutions can be assessed before implementation.

Bibliography

Ainley, M.; Mashayekhi, A.; Hicks, R.; Rahman, A. and Ravalia, A. 2007. *Islamic Finance in UK: Regulation and Challenges.* London: Financial Services Authority.

Baron, S. W. 1952. *A Social and Religious History of the Jews. Volume I: Ancient Times, Part I.* Jewish Publication Society of America.

Berger, A. 2004. *Encyclopedic Dictionary of Roman Law: Transactions of the American Philosophical Society*, New Ser. V. 43, Pt. 2. Clark, NJ, US: The Lawbook Exchange Ltd.

Blume, Fred. H. and Kearley, T. 2009. *Annotated Justinian Code* (2nd Edition). Available at: http://uwacadweb.uwyo.edu/blume%26justinian/. Access Date: 8 September 2017.

Calder(a), N. 2010. S͟harīa. In *Encyclopaedia of Islam* (2nd Edition). Edited by P. Bearman; Th. Bianquis; C. E. Bosworth; E. van Donzel and W. P. Heinrichs.

Brill Online. Durham University Library. Available at: http://www.brillonline.nl/subscriber/entry?entry=islam_COM-1040. Access Date: 6 August 2017.

Calder(b), N. 2010. *Uṣūl al- Fiḳh*. Encyclopaedia of Islam (2nd Edition). Edited by P. Bearman; Th. Bianquis; C. E. Bosworth; E. van Donzel and W. P. Heinrichs. Brill Online. Durham University Library. Available at: http://www.brillonline.nl/subscriber/entry?entry=islam_SIM-7761. Access Date: 6 August 2017.

Cassirer, E. 1979. *The Philosophy of the Enlightenment*. Princeton, NJ, US: Princeton University Press.

Catholic Encyclopedia. *Interest*. Available at: http://www.newadvent.org/cathen/08077a.htm. Access Date: 6 August 2017.

Catholic Encyclopedia. *Usury*. Available at: http://www.newadvent.org/cathen/15235c.htm. Access Date: 28 April 2018.

Donald, A. H. 1989. Christianity and Economics: Biblical Foundations. In *Economics and Religion* (Volume II). Edited by Paul Oslington, 89–179. Cheltenham: Edward Elgar Publishing Limited.

Donald, A. H. 2003. Christianity and Economics: Theological Ethics. In *Economics and Religion* (Volume II). Edited by Paul Oslington, 136–167. Cheltenham: Edward Elgar Publishing Limited.

Forrest, B. 2000. Methodological Naturalism and Philosophical Naturalism: Clarifying the Connection. *PHILO*, 3(2) (Fall–Winter), 7–29.

Friedman, H. H. 2001. The Impact of Jewish Values on Marketing and Business. *Journal of Macromaking*, 21(June), 74–81.

Friedman, L. W. and Friedman, H. H. 2009. *The Financial Meltdown of 2008: The Perspective of Jewish Law*. Available at: http://www.jlaw.com/Articles/resolving_estate_law.pdf. Access Date: 12 August 2017.

Grice-Hutchinson, M. 1978. *Early Economic Thought in Spain 1177–1740*. London, UK: George Allen & Unwin.

Hackett, L. 1992. *The Age of Enlightenment: The European Dream of Progress and Enlightenment*. Available at: http://history-world.org/age_of_enlightenment.htm. Access Date: 4 August 2018.

Heimann, E. 1947. *History of Economic Doctrines*. UK: Oxford University Press.

Hezser, C. 1993. *Form, Function, and Historical Significance of the Rabbinic Story in Yerushalmi Neziqin* (Texte und Studien zum antiken Judentum). Germany: Mohr Siebeck.

Hooker, R. 1996. *The European Enlightenment: The Scientific Revolution*. Available at: http://www.wsu.edu:8001/~dee/ENLIGHT/SCIREV.HTM. Access Date: 4 August 2017.

Huberman, L. 1937. *Man's Worldly Goods*. London: The Camelot Press Ltd.

Hunt, E. K. 1981. *Property and Prophets: The Evolution of Economic Institutions and Ideologies*. New York: Harper & Row.

Lannaccone, L. R. 1998. Introduction to the Economics of Religion. *Journal of Economic Literature*, XXXVI(September), 1465–1496.

Legal Week. 2009. *French Reform to Bring Islamic Finance at the Heart of Europe*. Available at: http://www.allbusiness.com/company-activities-management/company-structures/12596126-1.html. Access Date: 20 August 2017.

Leiter, M. S. *Jewish Law Research Guide*. Gables, FL, US: University of Miami. Available at: http://library.law.miami.edu/judaicguide.php#secondary. Access Date: 2 September 2017.

Maharal: Chapter 1: Mishna 1: Part 3. Available at: http://www.torah.org/learning/maharal/p1m1part3.html. Access Date: 23 January 2018.

Munby, D. L. 1956. *Christianity and Economic Problems*. London, UK: Macmillan & Co Ltd.

Neuser, J. 1972. *A History of the Jews in Babylonia* (Volume 4). Leiden, The Netherlands: E. J. Brill.

Numbers, R. L. Science Without God: Natural Laws and Christian Beliefs. In *When Science and Christianity Meet*. Edited by C. L. David and L. N. Ronald, 265–287. Chicago, IL, US: The University of Chicago Press.

Resnicoff, S. H. 2005. Contemporary Issues in Halakhah. In *Modern Judaism*. Edited by N. De Lange and M. Freud-Kandel, 363–374. UK: Oxford University Press.

Runzo, J. 2001. *A Short Introduction: Global Philosophy of Religion*. New York: One World Publication.

Ryan, P. M. A. 2003. *The History of the Market System*. Available at: http://www.zeromillion.com/econ/history-of-the-market-system.html. Access Date: 23 March 2017.

Schacht, R. 1985. *Nietzsche*. London: Taylor & Francis Ltd.

"Scientific Revolution," Microsoft Encarta Online Encyclopedia. 2009. Available at: http://encarta.msn.com/encyclopedia_701509067/Scientific_Revolution.html. Access Date: 4 August 2017.

The History of Economic Thoughts. Available at: http://homepage.newschool.edu/het/. Access Date: 21 July 2017.

The List: The World's Fastest Growing Religions. 2009. Available at: http://www.foreignpolicy.com/story/cms.php?story_id=3835. Access Date: 14 August 2017.

Wæver, O. 2007. World Conflict Over Religion: Secularism as Flawed Solution. Paper Presented at the Annual Meeting of the International Studies Association 48th Annual Convention, Hilton Chicago, Chicago, IL, USA. Available at: http://www.allacademic.com/meta/p181388_index.html. Access Date: 18 August 2017.

CHAPTER 2

Exploring the Epistemology of Utility Function in Islamic Economics: Foundation of Islamic Finance

Fawad Khaleel and Alija Avdukić

Key Topics

- Epistemology of Utility Function
- Faith and Utility
- Islamic Economics

1 Introduction

Islam manifests itself as a last and conclusive religious doctrine in the series of Abrahamic and pre-Abrahamic prophetic religions. It shares many common grounds with its Abrahamic cousins in the divine methods used in revelation, procedures of canonisation and approaches to authoritative interpretations and the transcendental prescription of recording oral and

F. Khaleel · A. Avdukić (✉)
Al-Maktoum College of Higher Education, Dundee, UK
e-mail: a.avdukic@almcollege.ac.uk

V. Efendic (ed.), *Islamic Finance Practices*,
https://doi.org/10.1007/978-3-030-34420-7_2

written traditions, with a difference: wherein Muslims employed slightly more rigorous concerns in solidifying and preserving the religious text by introducing sciences to document and preserve sacred texts. The Qur'an exhibits accounts of many previous prophets by annotating their interaction with people, thus illustrating their tormented experiences and expedient proficiency, in a calling to submit to Allah's will. This is epitomised within the connotation of the Arabic word, *Islam* (Salvatore 2007: 134). In the Islamic version of this process of divine revelations, each revealed doctrine confirmed and re-established the preceding ones. Islam being the last and final doctrine invalidated the previous ones and introduced a new set of rules called *shari'ah*. In all the revealed doctrines, the methods and rules of submission differed, although the principle of submission to Allah's will and the relationship status of creator to creation remained the same. Therefore, Islam claims that it did not introduce any new ideas, rather, it restored and created a renaissance for previously introduced morals, ethics and principles, along with re-establishing a relationship of creator and creation combined with the message of submission to Allah's will (Salvatore 2007: 134).

2 Concept of Utility in Islamic Economics

Admonishment in Islam is sourced from a contract between creator and creation, established in a time of pre-worldly existence. This contract sets the foundations of the relationship between the two, which is further recollected by announcing the concept of *fitra* (natural human nature). There are many indirect references to *fitra* (human nature) in the Qur'an, such as verses[1] [7:172–173], which are further elaborated in the *hadith,* for example (Sahih Muslim, Book No. 33, *Hadith* No. 6425):

> No child is born but upon *Fitra*. He then said. Recite: The nature made by Allah in which He created man, there is no altering of Allah's nature; that is the right religion.

[1] [7:172] (Recall) when your Lord brought forth their progeny from the loins of the children of 'Adam, and made them testify about themselves (by asking them,). Am I not your Lord?. They said, Of course, You are. We testify. (We did so) lest you should say on the Day of Judgment, We were unaware of this [7:173] or you should say, It was our forefathers who associated partners with Allah, and we were their progeny after them; would you then destroy us on account of what the erroneous did?

Human beings are created with *fitra* and 'there is never a change in the original nature created by Allah' (Qur'an, 30:30). Shah Wali Allah further suggests that *fitra* is a religious doctrine that has remained throughout the ages, and there is consensus from all the prophets regarding this (1996: 72). Creation has its state of *amr* (order, law) and the *amr* for humans is in their creation founded on *fitra*, through which they exhibit a built-in function for judgement and understanding of what is good and what is not. Due to human vulnerability and susceptibility to the devil's whispers and *nafs* (lower soul), they become dormant in righteousness and require a call, followed by continuous development to return to the natural state of *fitra*. Islam is considered as this call which is achieved through *furqan*[2] (the criterion). The Qur'an is a discourse on frames of action and interaction between Allah and humans, and between humans and other creation. The Qur'an is based on (Arkoun 2002: 566):

> Complex historical process engaging simultaneously [in] social, political..., cultural, and normative factors. These are [further] entangled with ritual, customs, ethics, familial structures [,]... the competing structures of the imagination and the collective interactive memory of... all cultural groups of the ancient Near East.

The Qur'an was revealed through *wahyi* (revelation) and was further elaborated by Muhammad the Prophet of Islam, through his behaviour, actions, response to other's actions and didactic sayings known as, *Sunnah*. These two sources create a skeleton structure for jurisprudence, law and regulations; however a review of the Qur'an reveals that it was neither intended to be and nor is 'an exhaustive catalogue of discrete exhortations and specific commands' (Salvatore 2007: 135). In Rahman's opinion, the Qur'an (as cited in Neuser and Sonn 1999: 60):

> Emerges as a document that from first to the last seeks to emphasize all those moral tensions that are necessary for creative human actions.

The Qur'an is a religious text, which also concentrates on the moral principles joined with some social and economic law. While the Qur'an combined with *hadith* introduces an under structure of legal axioms through

[2] *Furqaan* is one of the many names of Qur'an.

which Islamic law is built, its focus remains to elevate humans from minimum divine requirements, by building a society on systematic moral principles. The Qur'an has an axiomatic 'nexus between salvation and human action' (Salvatore 2007: 135). This nexus is facilitated by pronouncing the right human action,[3] along with the right attitude for that action, as an *ibada* (service to Allah). Human beings are accredited as witnesses of their own actions and they are motivated to contemplate guarding themselves against wrong human actions through the development of *taqwa* (God consciousness).

The Qur'an also outlines the capability of moral fluctuation in human beings. It lays the philosophical foundations of this abstruse idea in verse seventy-two of chapter thirty-three and in versus thirty to thirty-four of chapter two. Verse[4] seventy-two in chapter thirty-three demonstrates the unwillingness of creation to take Allah's trust, that is, the responsibility to obey Allah, subject to the condition of free will. Human beings took this responsibility in return for a reward, with the condition of fulfilment of trust. The verse goes further and points to human ignorance in taking of this trust. The condition of not knowing or being ignorant of trust can metamorphose by developing the understanding circumscribing the trust.

Chapter two verses thirty to thirty-four records a conversation between angels and Allah, in which angels elaborate upon the capacity of unjust actions in humans. In Islamic teachings, the angels by their nature are not capable of retaining, attaining or comprehending any knowledge or information other than what Allah has given them. Therefore, angels address their concerns based on what Allah has divulged. The conversation goes further and demonstrates a very key human proclivity, that is, by attaining divine knowledge, which is revealed to them, they can improve their status within Allah's creation and can reach a higher state of piety. Therefore, one of the key factors in a physical and practical return to the state of *fitra* is gaining knowledge and building comprehension of the type of actions required, based on revealed knowledge. However, converting the knowledge into intentions and further into actions requires an active role of

[3]This Qur'an guides to the most upright Way and gives good news to the believers who do right actions that they will have a large reward (17:9).

[4]Verily, We did offer the trust of compliance to the heavens, and the earth, and the mountains and they, being fearful, breach not what is entrusted upon them. Yet man, with his free will, is the only one who breaches this trust of compliance. For, verily, he wrongs himself without knowing it (33:72).

other key factors. Shah Wali Allah identifies two major forces in a human: they are *al-ruh al-tabiiyya* (natural forces) and *quwwa bahimiyya* (animalistic forces) (1996: 58). Natural force calls for the system of morals and principles as they emanate from the soul because of human creation on *fitra,* while the animalistic force is based on physical needs and these are similar in humans and animals. These two forces have separate individual perceptions and cognition of pleasure and pain, which can equally result in right or wrong human actions.

The fulfilment of physical needs or all animal instincts is not necessarily always wrong or evil. Similarly, all the acts of worship and attempts for striving are not always good or right as they could involve polytheism which to Islam is unjust. The type of result these two forces mutually or independently can produce depends on 'influence'. A human is under three kinds of major influences. The first is *nafs* (soul) which has many further sub-categories and classifications. Other than *nafs,* there is a conscience, and influence of whispers from Satan. These influences channel the two forces in humans either towards right human actions or wrong ones. For humans to return to state of *fitra* requires the forces to be in equilibrium. The state of equilibrium is when the two forces result in the actions of rightly guided people as mentioned in the Qur'an and *hadith.* Shah Wali Allah suggests that the state of *fitra* is composed of four key components: *tahara* (purity); *ikhbat* (humbleness towards Allah); *taqwa* (piety); and *adala* (justice) (1996: 157).

These components are part of a development journey, which is expatiated in numerous works, evinced by many scholars and further explicated in Nazim and Asutay's research work,[5] which is shown in Fig. 1 (2009: 87). The embarkation of the development starts from *tawhid* (Allah's unity/uniqueness/sovereignty) and each development stage accumulates from it (Zaman and Asutay 2009: 87). The second landmark is this development process is *fiqh* (Jurisprudence) followed by *adl* (Justice), *iman,*[6]

[5] For further reading on stages of development within Islam please consult: Nazim Zaman and Mehmet Asutay, 2009. Divergence Between Aspirations and Realities of Islamic Economics: A Political Economy Approach to Bridging the Divide. *IIUM Journal of Economics and Management* 17(1), 73–96.

[6] According to hadith, Iman is: "That you affirm Allah, His angels, His books, His messengers, and the Last Day, and that you affirm the Decree, the good of it and the bad of it".

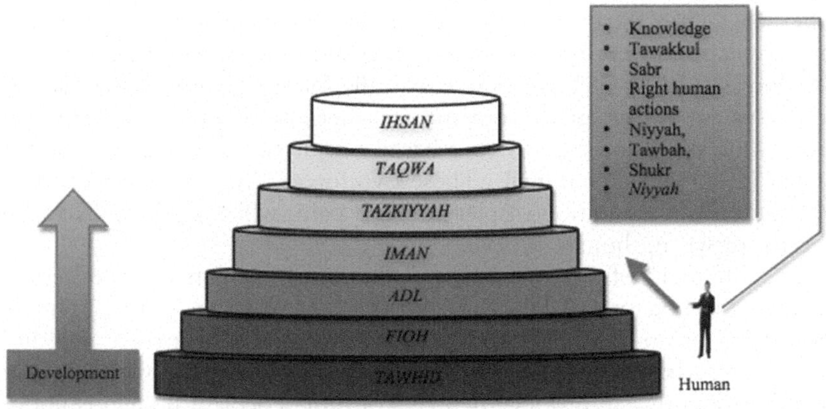

Fig. 1 Development journey in Islamic economics

tazkiyyah (Self purification), *taqwa* (God consciousness) and *Ihsan*[7] as a final 'finishing embellishment' (Zaman and Asutay 2009: 76). This is illustrated in Fig. 1.

The advancements in this journey of development are dependent on further factors. It requires the individual to build momentum and energy (EMD) which helps him or her to fulfil the requirements of his/her current development stage. When an individual fulfils the requirement, he or she progresses to the next stage. A level of EMD is required, even if one remains at one stage. The factors behind the build-up of momentum and energy can be infinite in numbers; however, the theological foundations for many of these factors have a recursive feature. When the potential of these factors is confined to the analytical observation and study, whereby, the process of constant progression in the life of the Prophet Muhammad is kept in view with the context in which Qur'an descended (*al-Asbab al-Nuzool*) in smithereens, it acts as vantage points. An analysis of these vantage points unfolds and elucidates certain key and vital development factors that build up the required momentum and energy. These vital and key development factors consist of two set of agents: one has a practical dimension, while the other subsumes the spiritual dimension. This is also

[7] According to hadith, Ihsan is: "That you worship Allah as if you see Him, for if you don't see Him then truly He sees you".

shown in Eq. (1), where 'EMC' refers to the level of momentum and energy, 'Set A' refers to a set of agents with practical dimensions, and 'Set B' refers to set of agents with spiritual dimensions.

$$\text{EMC} = \text{Set A} + \text{Set B} \tag{1}$$

The elements of Set A are: *ilm* knowledge; *tawakkul* (reliance); *sabr* (patience) and rightful human actions, while members of Set B consist of: *niyyah* (intention); *tawbah* (repentance) and *shukr* (a show of gratitude and acknowledgement).

As

$$\text{Set A} = \{Ilm, Tawakkul, Sabr, \text{ rightful human actions}\}$$

And

$$\text{Set B} = \{Niyyah, Tawbah, Shukr\}$$

Therefore:

$$\text{EMC} \approx \{Ilm, Tawakkul, Sabr, \text{ rightful human actions}\} + \{Niyyah, Tawbah, Shukr\} \tag{2}$$

Knowledge, as formerly explained, is a vital distinction, which allows humans to differentiate between good and bad; however, this alone cannot incapacitate human's capacity for unjust actions. Therefore, knowledge needs to be translated into rightful human actions. Al-Asafahaani in his work *Hilyatul Awliyaa* elaborates on this concept by quoting Abu Darda's saying (Pearl of Wisdom II, May 20, 2010):

> One does not become truly pious unless he becomes learned, and one does not enjoy the beauty and benefits of his knowledge unless he practices what he knows.

The Qur'an asserts the importance of rightful actions by dedicating more than a hundred and eighty-five verses to this matter. In these verses, it provides a clear distinction on the impacts of right and wrong human actions. Another factor with direct reciprocity to the correct human action is *niyyah* (Intention). Muhammad, the Prophet of Islam, pronounced the importance of *niyyah* by saying[8]: "Deeds are [a result] only of the intentions [of the actor], and an individual is [rewarded] only according to that which he intends" (Sahih Bukhari, 1[1]: No. 1).

At the core of every human action is *niyyah.* It is not only the act of judgement of righteousness in human actions, but it also has an imperative tendency that, it can increase, decrease or nullify the outcome of rightful human actions on an individual's development process. Besides *niyyah,* the wrongful human actions also influence the individual's development process, and any individual despite his/her progress within the development process is vulnerably prone to wrongful human actions. Although Qur'an associates believers with rightful human action[9] and nonbelievers with wrongful human actions,[10] it also at some places associates nonbelievers with the conduct of rightful human actions[11] and wrongful human conduct of actions[12] by believers. The Qur'an (2:35) while narrating the anecdote of Adam's exile from the heavens expatiates *tawbah* (repentance) as a key function, which differentiates between the intrinsic nature of righteousness and evilness. Adam and Satan both committed sins by acting unjustly, however, Adam resorted to *tawbah* (repentance), which was accepted by Allah and further facilitated the development process for Adam. The Qur'an through many other startling verses[13] draws attention towards this tool of regaining momentum for

[8] Sahih Bukhari, Vol 1, Book 1, Hadith No. 1.

[9] As for those who believe and do right actions, We will pay them their wages in full. Allah does not love wrongdoers (Quran, 3:57).

[10] They denied Our Signs, so Allah seized them for their wrong actions. Allah is fierce in retribution (Quran, 3:11).

[11] The metaphor of those who reject their Lord is that their actions are like ashes scattered by strong winds on a stormy day. They have no power at all over anything they have earned. That is extreme misguidance (Quran, 14:18).

[12] (Believers say): 'Our Lord, we heard a caller calling us to faith: "Believe in your Lord!" and we believed. Our Lord, forgive us our wrong actions, erase our bad actions from us and take us back to You with those who are truly good.' (Quran, 3:193) (His servants are) those who say: 'Our Lord, we believe, so forgive us our wrong actions and safeguard us from the punishment of the Fire' (Quran, 3:16).

[13] But as for those who do evil actions and then subsequently repent and believe, in that case your Lord is Ever-Forgiving, Most Merciful (Quran, 7:153).

You who believe! Repent to Allah. It may be that your Lord will erase your bad actions from you and admit you into Gardens (Quran, 66:8).

development. The Qur'an signifies and connotes this correlation between rightful human actions and *tawbah* by stating:

> Except for those who repent and believe and act rightly. They will enter the Garden and they will not be wronged in any way. (Qur'an, 19:60)

Ghazali expounds *tawbah* as "the first step of the aspirants…the prelude of the selection and election for those who are brought close to God" (Al-Ghazali 1990: 30). The necessary prerequisite and a condition for *tawbah* is the *niyyah*, state of remorse, knowledge of wrong and an imperative intention to correct what is wrong, along with the feeling of guilt and regret for past wrongful actions, followed by a determination and an intention to abstain from what is wrong and opt for high moral and righteous conduct in future (Al-Ghazali 1990: 30). The above prerequisite knowledge allows the individual to realise the practice of wrongful human action and enables him/her to rectify and/or abstain from it. When the act of *tawbah* fulfils all the required conditions, it may elicit a call of response from Allah.

From the 99 names of Allah mentioned in the Qur'an, two specific names explain particular virtues of forgiveness and mercy through which Allah responses to the calls of those who repent. These names are: *at-Tawwab (acceptor of Repentance)* and *ar-Rahim (most merciful)*. Allah's attribute of *at-Tawwab* and *ar-Rahim* 'expresses the manifestation of grace' in response to human actions (Chaghatai 2006: 1165). What adds to the above discourse in this context is also widely apparent in the Qur'an (25:71),[14] where the action of righteous conduct calls for the divine response of *tawbah*. The virtue of grace as a pivotal intrinsic value enables the development of momentum, which together with *tawakkul* (reliance) and *sabr* (patience) forms an important part in the appreciation of this intrinsic development. The Qur'an reflects on this: 'Only those who are patient shall receive their reward in full, without reckoning' (39:10). The Qur'an mentions *tawakkul*[15] numerous times and elaborates on the virtues it possesses in attracting divine grace and acts as a tool capable of producing a reactionary manifestation of grace from Allah. The manifestation of divine grace comes with a requisite, that the individual in

[14] Allah is Ever-Forgiving, Most Merciful-for certainly all who repent, and act rightly have turned sincerely towards Allah (Quran, 25:70–71).

[15] Whoever relies on Allah (has Tawakkul), He is sufficient for him (Quran, 65:3).

exchange offers *shukr* (thanksgiving), as illustrated in the verse[16] (2:52). *Shukr* further triggers a divine response of re-compensation, as explicitly mentioned in verse[17] (3:145). The more these variables are inflated, the more an individual develops.

The collective force of all these intrinsic factors provides the momentum required, for progressing through development stages. A decrease or underdevelopment of one or more of these factors can cause retrogression and can abate or even negate the effects of other factors, which may result in downgrading within the hierarchy of development stages. However, an increase cannot be even or linear along the whole range of factors. The balance in increase within members of 'Set A' depends directly on an individual's circumstances. The circumstances equal the endurance and capacity of the individual, as mentioned in Qur'an[18] (02:285). Hence, it suggests that: endurance and capacity of the individual sets the benchmark for elements of set 'A'. The elements of 'Set B' play an equal part as do members of 'Set A'; however, they are purely of a metaphysical nature and pose asomatous characteristics, therefore, neither they nor a standard for them can figuratively or literally be quantified, although to progress in development stages there exists a non-quantifiable benchmark (NB) for members of 'Set B'.

Each Muslim is at one of the development stages and to progress to the next level requires all the elements of 'Set B' to be on or above the invisible benchmark along with all the elements of 'Set A' to be on or above the 'capacity'. The elements of 'Set A' can be over the capacity, when he/she outperforms as compared to what his/her circumstances allow. The 'Fig. 2' demonstrates an example, where an individual 'Y' has an excess knowledge while he is required to build a history of 'right human actions' along with increase in *sabr* and *tawakul.* Once all elements of Set A and B reach the required level, all the requirements of the current development stage are executed, and the individual 'Y' can then progress onto the next stage. After progression individual 'Y' might become more aware of further 'opportunities for performance'. This awareness could

[16] Then We pardoned you after that so that perhaps you would show thanks (Quran, 2:52).

[17] We will recompense the thankful (Quran, 3:145).

[18] God does not burden/impose a self except its endurance/capability (Quran, 02:285).

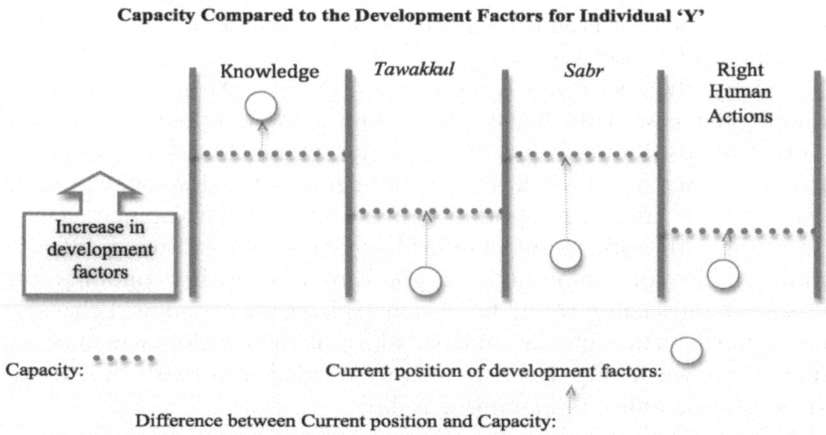

Fig. 2 Capacity development in Islamic economics

redefine circumstances and as a result enlarges capacity, and in this manner, the new standard for further progression will be set.

'Opportunities for performance' are simply the junctures where a Muslim can seek pleasure of Allah. Qur'an (9:72)[19] designates the pleasure of Allah as an ultimate achievement. To further elaborate on the 'opportunities for performance', consider the example of individual 'X'. Individual 'X' is at the second development stage that is *fiqh*, who, after expanding the elements of Set A and Set B, executes all the requirements of the second stage and progresses on to *Adl*. At this point, individual 'X' is already fulfilling all the requirements of *fiqh*. However, on reaching the stage of *Adl*, he/she realises that there is a wider responsibility towards rectifying social injustice. On this realisation, individual 'X' has a choice to either act, and endeavour to establish justice; or ignore this realisation. The realisation and willingness to act requires a different type and level of knowledge: *tawakkul*, *sabr*, rightful human actions, *niyyah*, *tawbah* and *shukr*. These levels set the new standards and benchmarks, while the realisation of the need to rectify injustice provides an awareness of further 'opportunities for performance'. If individual 'X' chooses not to act, he/she will slip down to the previous level. However, the *maqasid al*

[19] Best of all is Allah's goodly pleasure; that is the grand achievement (Quran, 09:72).

shari'ah (purpose of Islamic law) will define which decision for individual 'X' is appropriate and advisable.

Similarly, the social and economic actions of a Muslim also largely depend on the scenario he/she faces during the development journey. In other words, the difference between the set benchmark and values of members of Set A and Set B; the requirements of the development stage along with the current position of individual within development stages; translate into the satisfaction an individual gets from performing different actions and by consuming different goods or services. In economics, the measure of satisfaction is 'utility', which explains the economic behaviour of individuals. Through the understanding of the development process, utility as shown in Eq. 1 can be further divided into two major forms that is: holistic utility and atomistic utility.

$$\text{Utility} = \text{Atomistic Utility} + \text{Holistic Utility} \tag{3}$$

Atomistic utility is a natural inclination, or a propensity based on the utilitarian philosophical concept of pain and pleasure. Bentham suggests that these innate natural forces 'point out what we ought to do, as well as to determine what we shall do' (Bentham 1948: 1). Holistic utility is the perception of an individual based on the following: the increase across the members of Set 'A' and Set 'S' required to reach a benchmark; along with an individual's current position in the development stages and requirements of current development stage. The nature of *fitra,* in humans, instigates towards the continuous development, however, *nafa* and other external influences can exert negative effects on this instigation. In every human, the ratio between instigation and negative factors (*nafs* and other external factors) determine the individual's willingness for development. This further translates into the values of elements of Set A and B, which interpret the 'holistic utility' an individual receives from specific good or services. Fluctuation in all the above factors can result in different 'holistic utility' for different goods and services. The aggregate of 'atomistic utility' and 'holistic utility' forms the correlation with want or desire.

'Holistic utility' is the concept that encompasses this world, the Hereafter and the Judgement Day, for instance, based on the assumption that the consumption of product 'x' is prohibited religiously. This means that the product 'x' does have an atomistic utility, however, its consumption is classified as a sinful act which makes the aggregate 'holistic utility' zero or negative. Therefore, while a utility can be positive within an atomistic framework, however, the same utility when perceived from the ideology of 'holistic utility' can turn the aggregate into a negative, making the aggregate zero or negative. It could be suggested that, when the aggregate of atomistic and holistic utility turns into a negative value, the individual develops a hatred towards that thing and perceives it as something, which does more harm than good. The higher an individual goes in the developmental stages, the larger the difference between the holistic and atomistic utility becomes. This line of argument can also be used to explain the consumer behaviour from Islamic economics perspective.

The literature in 'Islamic Economics' presents discombobulating views on utility. The general view of Islamic economists is that our rationale only helps us to pursue atomistic utility. The reason our rationale is insufficient, is because we only possess information regarding the physical world. This understanding is also reflected in the categorisation of knowledge acknowledged by classical scholars and presented by Usmani. He makes claims about the categorisations stating: 'Each one of them has a definite range and fixed sphere of activity beyond which it does not work' (Usmani 2007: 32). The first two are the knowledge gained through senses and knowledge gained through intellect, however, these two factors do not provide us with the information needed to understand and pursue holistic utility. Therefore, Usmani argues that the 'Wahy' (Divine Revelations) are sent to enlighten us about the third type of knowledge, which we cannot perceive on our own (Usmani 2007: 33). In the Torah, the laws categorised as *chukim* and *mitzvoth* are also considered threads from a similar fabric of knowledge. The third type of knowledge is rationalised as the knowledge which provides the information required to acknowledge our covenant with Allah, and if we choose to do so, then it presents the methodology that we can use to maximise utility in a controlled manner by applying the prescribed methods of increasing holistic utility. Furthermore, believing in a religious philosophy reflects an act of following the principles approved by that religious philosophy and rejecting the actions negated by the philosophy. The factors that permit one to do so are considered as the third type of knowledge.

There are many individuals who do not follow Islamic religious philosophy and lack the third type of knowledge. Therefore, they should not possess 'holistic utility', and neither withstand elements of Set A and B with a positive value. However, the present state of the world and a survey of history proves otherwise. Human beings who do not approve of

Islamic religious philosophy show clear signs of 'holistic utility' in their actions and consumption; therefore, it would be to disproportionate to assume that individuals outside the Islamic development stages are unable to accumulate any 'holistic utility'.

Holistic utility is the expression of 'good', and transcendental sources of Islam show a clear distinction between two types of good. One is referred to as '*khair*', while the other is classified as '*maroof*'. The *hadith*[20] (*Sahih al Bukhari, Kitab al Munaqib*: 3493) which designates the word '*khair*' with individuals who performed good actions, while being outside the fold of Islam; along with the verse[21] (3:110) which assigns *maroof* as a unique attribute of a Muslim community; explicates into a framework of two tiers of 'good'. In this framework, *khair* may be suggested as general good present in the entire humankind, which may stem from *fitra* and it could be the source of natural law; while *maroof* is the known good, and revelation is the source which allows human beings to know, this known good. Therefore, individuals outside the fold of Islam can develop *khair*, which in return could stimulate some of the variables in holistic utility. For such an individual, who although does not approve of Islamic religious philosophy and lacks the third type of knowledge, hence is deficient of a known good that is: *maroof*; however, he or she can still generate positive values within some of the variables of EMC, by stimulating good that is: *khair*, which originates in form from *fitra*; as demonstrated in Fig. 3.

Therefore, through the right application of intellect, the production of 'right human actions' and *sabr* can arise, while the motivation and guidance underpinning them may bourgeon from *khair*, with its roots in *fitra*. The singularity of existence of *fitra*, in all human beings could also be the reason for similarities in normative ethics across different cultures and regions, around the world. However, according to an Islamic theological position, the disassociation of these human beings with Islamic religious philosophy results in no meaningful value for other development factors like *Tawakkul*, *Niyyah*, *Tawbah* and *Shukr*. Consequently, the positive value for 'right human actions' and *sabr* does not translate into any momentum and energy (EMC), which could be utilised to rise in the

[20] People good at the time of ignorance, will remain good after accepting Islam (Sahih al Bukhari: Kitab al Munaqib, 3493).

[21] Ye are the best community that hath been raised up for mankind. Ye enjoin right conduct and forbid (Quran, 3:110).

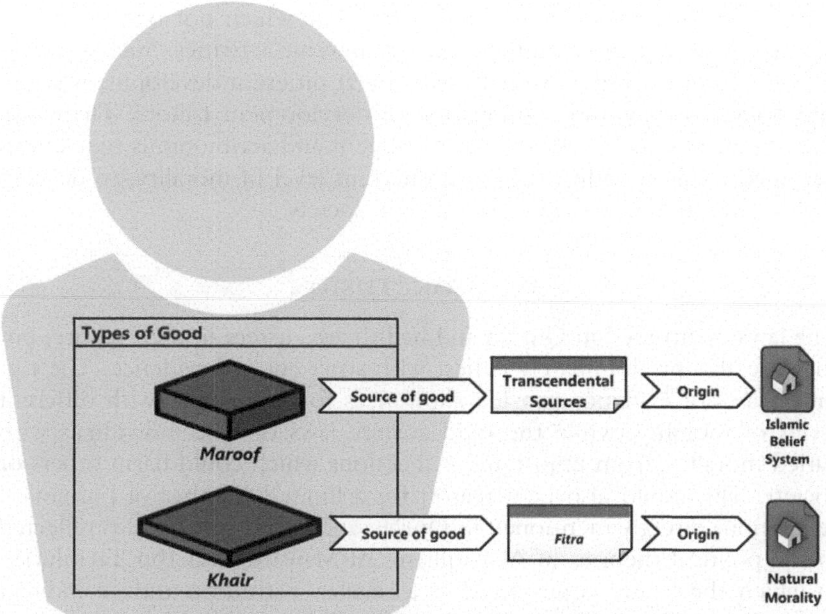

Fig. 3 Types of good, in intention, decision and action of humans

hierarchy of development stages. The Qur'an explains this within the following verse (14:18):

> The metaphor of those who reject their Lord is that their actions are like ashes scattered by strong winds on a stormy day. They have no power at all over anything they have earned. That is extreme misguidance.

Therefore, the process of development is dependent on the theological requirements, because of this, the first development stage and the foundation stone for further development is considered as *tawhid*. Furthermore, the theological basis for striving by performing correct human actions combined with the self-realisation of a need for development, purposeful obedience and a continuous struggle of self-guarding against wrongful human actions, along with the acknowledgement of inability to succeeded without alliance, assistance and the will of Allah, acts as a structure of joist to percolate a just and congenial society which not only generates but also nurtures moral and just socio-economic activities. Such a society is made up of diverse individuals who are at different development stages and possess a manifold combination of development factors. Therefore, Islam regulates such a society with stringent and acrimonious regulations designed to allow individuals with different level of morality, to develop without causing any harm or injustice in society.

3 Conclusion

The laws mentioned in Qur'an and hadith are austere in their nature, but they are also predominately behest with strict laws of evidence. The rigorous laws of evidence provide allowances for individuals with different levels of morality, while the rigid austere laws obviate individuals with varied morality, from unjust and evil actions which could harm others or society. This could also be a reason for a limited number of puritanical regulations directly mentioned in Qur'an and hadith, and is also reflected in the political theories of Al-Baqillani, Al-Mawardi and Ibn Taymiyyah, in which the 'state' is perceived as a secular institution and an indirect expression of Islam (Lapidus 1996: 19), while the direct expression of Islam is through the community of Muslim scholars and holy men. The laws and regulations of the state, although they could stem from *shari'ah*, however, its institutional enforcement should be limited to the explicit transcendental laws directly subscribed in Qur'an or hadith. These laws only prevent individuals possessing various levels of morality, from vitiating the society, while the advocacy for development is to be provided by the holy men and Muslim scholars.

Market regulations fall under the same category outlined above. Therefore, the market regulations enforced by the state should be limited to the explicit transcendental laws directly subscribed in Qur'an or hadith. The development of society and markets, within an Islamic framework, should be conducted by the holy man and scholars; as they can directly influence the factors behind holistic utility. Moreover, the dictums, legal maxims and moral aphorisms concerning regulations are divinely constituted and possess wider areas of engagement, and if in the process of implementing them, these dictums, legal maxims and moral aphorisms are narrowed so as to contextualise them with the issues concerning the market and the society, there is a possibility that the process of contextualising could create laws, which may hinder the development of individuals at lower levels of development stages, by adversely effecting the factors required for development. In such a case, the society may end up having a minority of individuals with high levels of holistic utility, alongside an underdeveloped majority with higher level of atomistic utility.

Bibliography

Al-Ghazali, A. H. M. I. M. 1990. *Al-Ghazzali on Repentance Book Thirty-One of the Revival of the Religious Sciences.* Translated from Arabic by Martin S. Stern. Pakistan: Vanguard.

Ainley, M., Mashayekhi, A., Hicks, R., Rahman, A., and Ravalia, A. 2007. *Islamic Finance in UK: Regulation and Challenges.* London: Financial Services Authority.

Arkoun, M. 2002. Islam. In *Encyclopaedia of the Quran*, Volume 2, edited by J. D. McAuliffe, 565–570. Leiden and Boston: Brill.

Asutay, M. 2007. A Political Economy Approach to Islamic Economics: Systemic Understanding for an Alternative Economic System. *Kyoto Bulletin of Islamic Area Studies* 1(2), 3–18.

Bentham, J. 1948. *An Introduction to the Principles of Morals and Legislation.* New York: Hafner.

Blume, F. H., and Kearley, T. 2009. *Annotated Justinian Code*, 2nd edition. Available at http://uwacadweb.uwyo.edu/blume%26justinian/. Access Date 8 September 2017.

Bukari, M. B. I. 1999. *Sahih al Bukhari: Kitab al Munaqib. Dar-ussalam.* Saudi Arabic: Riyaz.

Campion, M. A., Medsker, G. J., and Higgs, A. C. 1993. Relations Between Work Group Characteristics and Effectiveness: Implications for Designing Effective Work Groups. *Personnel Psychology* 46(4) (Winter), 823–850.

Chaghatai, M. I. 2006. *Muhammad Asad: Europe's Gift to Islam*, Volume 2. Pakistan: Sang-e-Meel Publications.

Chapra, M. U. 1992. *Islam and the Economics Challenge.* Leicester: The Islamic Foundation.

Donald A. H. 1989. Christianity and Economics: Biblical Foundations. In *Economics and Religion*, Volume 2, edited by Paul Oslington, 89–179. Cheltenham: Edward Elgar.

Ekelund, Robert, B. Jr., and Hebert, R. F. 1990. *A History of Economics Theory and Methods*, 3rd edition. New York, NY: McGraw-Hill.

Forrest, B. 2000. Methodological Naturalism and Philosophical Naturalism: Clarifying the Connection. *PHILO* 3(2) (Fall–Winter), 7–29.

Harris, E. M. 2003. Law and Economy in Classical Athens: [Demosthenes] Against Dionysodorus in Athenian Law in Its Democratic Context. In *Demos Classical Athenian Democracy: A Consortium for Electronic Publication in the Humanities*, edited by L. Adriaan, C. W. Blackwell, A. Mahoney, and A. Scaife. Available at http://www.stoa.org/projects/demos/article_law_economy?page=3&greekEncoding. Access date 11 September 2017.

Islahi, A. A. 1988. *Economic Concepts of Ibn Taimiyah*. Leicester: Islamic Foundation.

Janisch, H. N. 1979. *The Regulatory Process of the Canadian Transport Commission*. Ottawa: Supply and Services.

Lannaccone, L. R. 1998. Introduction to the Economics of Religion. *Journal of Economic Literature* XXXVI, 1465–1496.

Lapidus, I. M. 1996. State and Religion in Islamic Societies. *Present and Past* 151(1), 3–27.

Mander, W. J. 2005. Life and Finite Individuality: The Bosanquet/Pringle-Pattison Debate. *British Journal for the History of Philosophy* 13(1), 111–130.

Munby, D. L. 1956. *Christianity and Economic Problems*. London: Macmillan.

Neuser, J., and Sonn, T. 1999. *Comparing Religion Through Law: Judaism and Islam*. London: Routledge.

Numbers, R. L. 2010. Science Without God: Natural Laws and Christian Beliefs. In *When Science and Christianity Meet*, edited by C. L. David and L. N. Ronald, 265–287. Chicago, IL: University of Chicago Press.

Pearl of Wisdom II. Available at http://www.lutonmuslims.co.uk/Pearls2.htm#P25 Access Date 20 May 2016.

Regulatory Law 2010. Available at http://www.accesstolaw.com/index.php?option=com_content&view=category&layout=blog&view2=listing&id=78. Access Date 5 January 2016.

Salvatore, Armando. 2007. *The Public Sphere: Liberal Modernity, Catholicism, Islam*. New York, UK: Palgrave Macmillan.

Usmani, M. T. 2007. *An Approach to the Quranic Sciences: Uloom-ul-Quran*. Pakistan: Darul-Ishaat.

Wade, H. W. R. 1949. Quasi-Judicial' and Its Background. *The Cambridge Law Journal* 10(2), 216–240.

Wali Allah, S. 1996. *The Conclusive Argument from God: Shah Wali Allah of Delhi's Hujjat Allah al-Baligha*. Translated from Arabic by Marcia K. Hermansen. Leiden, The Netherlands: Brill.

Welngast, B. R. 1995. The Economic Role of Political Institutions: Market-Preserving Federalism and Economic Development. *Journal of Law, Economics & Organisation* 11(1), 1–31.

Wolff, J. 2006. *An Introduction to Political Philosophy*. Oxford: Oxford University Press.

Zaman, N. and Asutay, M. 2009. Divergence Between Aspirations and Realities of Islamic Economics: A Political Economy Approach to Bridging the Divide. *IIUM Journal of Economics and Management* 17(1), 73–96.

CHAPTER 3

Islamic Approach to Corporate Social Responsibility in Scientific Research with CSR Overview in Banking Sector of Bosnia and Herzegovina

Aida Hanić and Velid Efendic

Key Topics

- Islamic Approach to Corporate Social Responsibility
- Corporate Social Responsibility in Bosnia and Herzegovina
- The Use of Databases as a Scientific Tool

A. Hanić (✉)
Institute of Economic Sciences, Belgrade, Serbia
e-mail: aida.hanic@ien.bg.ac.rs

V. Efendic
School of Economics and Business, University of Sarajevo, Sarajevo, Bosnia and Herzegovina
e-mail: velid.efendic@efsa.unsa.ba

V. Efendic (ed.), *Islamic Finance Practices*,
https://doi.org/10.1007/978-3-030-34420-7_3

1 Introduction

The responsibility of business toward society is a phenomenon that still occupies a significant place in theory and practice. Its roots can be tracked down to 1920s where according to Krooss (1970), businessmen were seen as authority in matters like economy, politics, and even aesthetic which can be considered as the beginning of the development of the concept of corporate social responsibility. The need for institutionalization is a result of the internalization of common values, norms, and behaviors by members in a society (Mayhew 1982).

In the aspect of formal writing about corporations and its responsibilities toward society, we associate it with the period of 1930s. This particularly refers to writing of E. Merrick Dodd Jr and his paper titled "*For Whom Are Corporate Managers Trustees?*" which emphasizes that "*not only that business has responsibilities to the community but that our corporate managers who control business should voluntarily and without waiting for legal compulsion manage it in such a way as to fulfill those responsibilities*" (Dodd 1932).

From this period, Carroll (1999) lists writings done by Chester Barnard (1938) and his "*The Functions of the Executive*", J. M. Clark's (1939) "*Social Control of Business*", and Theodore Kreps' (1940) "*Measurement of the Social Performance of Business.*"

Although there were writings about corporate social responsibility, as a term, as a definition, and as a way of doing business it wasn't recognized before the 1950s. In 1951, Frank Abrams, chairman of the board of Standard Oil of Jersey stated that "*businessman as professionals have responsibilities to many groups besides themselves and their shareholders*" (Fredrick 2006). In academic sense, the term "*social responsibility*" was introduced by Howard Bowen in 1953 defining it in way that it "*refers to the obligations of businessmen to pursue those policies, to make those decisions, or to follow those lines of action which are desirable in terms of the objectives and values of our society*" (Bowen 1953).

The period after 1950s is the area when academic research starts with different approaches to corporate social responsibility. This is important to notice because corporate social responsibility doesn't have a unique definition. Votaw (1973) quoted by Carroll (1999) notes that "*the term (social responsibility) is a brilliant one; it means something, but not always the same thing, to everybody. To some it conveys the idea of legal responsibility or liability; to others, it means socially responsible behavior in an ethical sense; to still others, the meaning transmitted is that of "responsible for," in a causal mode; many simply equate it with a charitable contribution; some take it to mean socially conscious; many of those who embrace it most fervently see it as a mere synonym for "legitimacy," in the context of "belonging" or being proper or valid; a few see it as a sort of fiduciary duty imposing higher standards of behavior on businessmen than on citizens at large*".

In this aspect, Dahlsrud (2008) identified 37 different definitions of corporate social responsibility. This indicates that the concept evolved and became one of the most used terms in modern business. In this research, we choose the definition given by Kotler and Lee (2005) who defines corporate social responsibility as "*a commitment to improve community well-being through discretionary business practices and contributions of corporate resources.*" In other words, we can say that the focus is on the expectations of the stakeholders.

This definition can be observed as an "*American*" in terms of its origin and the values that it represents. Beside this way of understanding the corporate social responsibility, we also chose the definition given by the European Commission where corporate social responsibility is defined "*as the responsibility of enterprises for their impact on society*" (European Commission 2011). From these two different definitions, we can conclude that in the US corporate social responsibility maintained its voluntary character while in Europe it goes into the legal framework. This observation of different definitions of corporate social responsibility can also serve as a starting point in terms of the level of development of corporate social responsibility in business and scientific research.

However, it must be noted that the expectations of the public changed which led to a growing number of publications dealing with this concept and its use in various areas of business. On the other hand, the corporate social responsibility was and still is related with other terms especially with business ethics.

Depending the period of its development, corporate social responsibility was considered:

- Irrelevant, where the focus is on applying the free market principle to maximize profit for shareholders. Milton Freedman stated that "*there is one and only one social responsibility of business - to use its resources and engage in activities designed to increase its profits so long*

as it stays within the rules of the game, which is to say, engages in open and free competition without deception or fraud" (Friedman 1970).
- as a moral and social guideline for the business: Archie B. Carroll (1979, 1991) developed a pyramid of corporate social responsibility claiming that four kinds of social responsibilities composite total CSR: *economic* (be profitable), *legal* (obey the law), *ethical* (be ethical), and *philanthropic* (be a good corporate citizen).

Although corporate social responsibility is mainly associated with the company's activities toward society, during the time the question of the impact of corporate social responsibility on financial performances of business entities was asked. As a result, a number of researches have been done in that aspect, which emphasizes that corporate social responsibility gains importance also in the financial aspect.

As mentioned before, the corporate social responsibility has been an area of discussion not only for managers and organizations but management scholars and researches as well. In this paper, we decided to explore the level of representation of the Islamic approach to corporate social responsibility in scientific research. Why is this question important?

First, Islam as a set of moral, ethical, and social values is consistent of the:

- relationship between man and the Creator known as faith (arab. Aqidah), where humans are seen as trustees because everything belongs to the Creator,
- transformation and manifestation of faith known as law (arab. Shariah[1]) and
- moral determination of the individual (arab. Ahlak).

In that aspect, Islam defines the behavior of an individual and a business organization toward society ("*If you disclose your charitable expenditures, they are good; but if you conceal them and give them to the poor, it is better for you, and He will remove from you some of your misdeeds [thereby].*

[1] Great Islamic Scholar, Ibn al-Qayim, quoted in Auda (2007) states that Sharia is "*based on wisdom and achieving people's welfare in this life and the afterlife. Sharia is all about justice, mercy, wisdom, and good. Thus, any ruling that replaces justice with injustice, mercy with its opposite, common good with mischief, or wisdom with nonsense, is a ruling that does not belong to the Sharia, even if it is claimed to be so according to some interpretation.*"

And Allah, with what you do, is [fully] acquainted" Qur'an; 2:271) which means that Islamic approach to corporate social responsibility is different because it is derived from the Qur'an and Sunnah. Essentially, it shows that corporate social responsibility is considered to be an integral part of the Sharia which leads to the conclusion that Islamic approach to corporate social responsibility is older than conventional because it is old as religion itself.

The best example of responsibilities toward society is Zakat. Hayat and Malik (2014) define Zakat as a social welfare tax in terms that it is an annual tax on surplus income and wealth of Muslims and is equivalent to 2.5% of net worth in general. ("*So I have warned you of a fire which is blazing. None will [enter to] burn therein except the most wretched one, who had denied and turned away, but the righteous one will avoid it. [He] who gives [from] his wealth to purify himself and not [giving] for anyone who has [done him] a favor to be rewarded but only seeking the countenance of his Lord, Most High and he is going to be satisfied.*" Qur'an; 92:14–21.) Beside Zakat, charity (Sadaqah) or charitable payment is also very important in Islam and an example of social awareness.

Islam also has a concept of what is permitted (halal) and what is not permitted (haram). This is a guidance of how to act toward society and how to be responsible as an individual and as a corporation. Usmani (2002) notes that, according to Sharia rules, the company's activities can't be contrary to the moral values of the society. Author Sharani (2004) considers that Islamic financial institutions are reliable and optimistic about corporate social responsibility implementation.

Second, most of the literature from this area is based on Western values and ways of doing business which doesn't give a different perspective of corporate social responsibility and its meaning to the business organizations. Frederick (2006) states that "*the moral underpinnings of CSR are neither clear nor agreed upon.*" In Islam, there is no difference between the sacred and the profane. Because of these special characteristics of Islamic approach to business, corporate social responsibility observed in this manner can be a very interesting field of research. But the question is, is it?

This research is based on data retrieved from Scopus, which is considered to be the largest abstract and citation database of peer-reviewed literature and Web of Sciences (WoS), with an access to over 18,000 high impact journals. According to Guz and Rushchitsky (2009), WoS and

Scopus are the most widespread databases on different scientific fields. The period of analysis was from 1990 to 2017.

Bibliometric methods have been used for providing quantitative analysis of written publications where this type of analysis is based on the identification of the corpus of literature, i.e., publications in their broadest sense, within a given subject area (Ellegaard and Wallin 2015). In other words, it gives us a link between the searched term, authors, and published documents.

To do this analysis, we decided to use the term "*Corporate social responsibility and Islam*" as well as the short form "*CSR and Islam.*" Some authors like Khurshid et al. (2014) use the term "*Islamic corporate social responsibility*" or "*Islamic CSR*" so we also decided to include it in our analysis. Beside these above-mentioned terms, we also included business ethics, especially "*Islamic business ethics*" because business ethics and social responsibility are often used to refer to the same argument or code (Goel and Ramanathan 2014).

The research questions addressed in this research are defined as follows:

1. Is the Islamic approach to corporate social responsibility sufficiently present in the research?
2. Is there an interest in exploring the Islamic approach to corporate social responsibility? If yes, how much attention is paid to this field in scientific research? If not, what are the causes of insufficient research in this area on a global scale?
3. In which countries/regions is this research most represented?

This analysis can give a closer look to the level of representation of Islamic approach to corporate social responsibility and to show if there is an editorial interest to publish papers in this area. In this paper, we provide descriptive statistics that includes: number of publications per year, country of publication, and affiliation.

2 Islamic Approach to Corporate Social Responsibility

Islam appears to me like a perfect work of architecture. All its parts are harmoniously conceived to complement and support each other; nothing is superfluous and nothing lacking; and the result is a structure of absolute balance and solid composure. (Muhammad Assad)

Corporate scandals, international character of modern business and higher public expectations, influenced that companies need to behave more ethically. In terms of definition, we can say that ethics signifies the perception of society about of what is good and what is bad. In the aspect of business, Lenk (1996) states that today it is considered a necessary corrective behavior in the business world, which, within the framework of market freedom, should enable that society doesn't bear the consequences of the decisions that companies make, and will not be at the expense of society development. It is a normative field because it prescribes what an individual should do or should abstain from doing. Business ethics sometimes refers to the ethics of management or the organization's ethics since it is limited to a framework within organizations (Beekun 1996).

The period of 1960s is related to the development of business ethics, where according to De George (1982) the USA becomes the dominant economic force and where Americans multinational companies gain importance in the business world. In scientific aspect, business ethics begins to develop in 1970 when in 1974 the first scientific conference was held at the University of Kansas. The "founding father" of business ethics is considered to be Norman Bowie.

Because the question of ethics in business became important issue and more relevant, it led to the increasing number of research done in this area where according to Ismail and Zali (2014) the terms of religious aspects, business environment, business legislation, and business corporate responsibility were mostly represented. Ramasamy et al. (2010) note that thanks to corporate social responsibility the image of companies has been very popular among consumers.

One important aspect that needs to be considered is the influence of religion on company's business and relationship with the society. Religion is closely related to values and can have significant influence on consumer's attitude toward companies but also it can affect the company's business model. Brammer et al. (2007) note that organized religion plays a significant role in establishing and disseminating moral and ethical prescriptions where, according to Frederick (1998) it can influence organizational decision-making and workplace behavior.

In the aspect of relationship between religion, values, corporate social responsibility, and business ethics, several researches were done; Brammer et al. (2007), Ramasamy et al. (2010), and Jamali and Sidani (2013). An example of codifying the influence of religion on business is the "*Interfaith Declaration:* A *Code of Ethics on International Business for Christians, Muslims, and Jews*" with the aim to unite the shared moral, ethical, and spiritual values that are inherent in the common Abrahamic tradition. The Declaration (1994) found four common key concepts of Christianity, Islam, and Judaism that are applicable to business: justice (fairness), mutual respect (love and consideration), stewardship (trusteeship), and honesty (truthfulness).

According to Naqvi (1981), Islam is a philosophy of the "right" and the "right" can be viewed through the application of four basic axioms:

a. *Tahweed* (Unity of God—Say, "*To Allah belongs [the right to allow] intercession entirely. To Him belongs the dominion of the heavens and the earth. Then to Him you will be returned.*" Qur'an; 39–44). Badawi (2001) states that this approach represents the focus of Islamic thinking. It is a guide to achieve socioeconomic justice, moral action, and responsible business because it will have an impact on the entire organization that claims to be an Islamic;
b. *Equilibrium* which, according to Asutay (2007), means maintaining a balance between present needs and those in the future. On the other hand, Nasution (2009) states that the balance basically reflects the horizontal perspective of human life in order to complete the dimension of unity as a vertical perspective;
c. *Free will*, which essentially represents the goal of the Islamic economic system—to guarantee individual freedom and freedom of choice of opportunity. Naqvi (2003) states that although individuals have the freedom of choice in terms of the road they want to follow, they also have a responsibility toward themselves, society, and the Creator;
d. *Responsibility*, that relates to previously mentioned axioms because the responsibility is closely related to each act by the individual's actions. This suggests responsibility for the benefit of the wider community (Asutay 2007) not only through a set of voluntary activities but also through mandatory ones to ensure that social interest can actually be achieved.

In addition to the above four axioms, there are three basic characteristics of the Islamic approach to corporate social responsibility: *justice (arab. Adl)* where according to Iqbal and Mirakhor (2011) the main goal of Islam is to create just and moral social order through human agency (Say: "*My Lord has ordered justice,*" Qur'an; 7:29), *trust (arab. Amanet)* ("*O you who have believed, do not betray Allah and the Messenger or betray your trusts while you know [the consequence],*" Qur'an; 8:27), and charity (*arab. Ihsan*). Umar ud din (1991), quoted by Beekun and Badawi (2005), defines Ihsan as "*an act which benefits persons other than those from whom the act proceeds without any obligation*" ("*Indeed, Allah orders justice and good conduct and giving to relatives and forbids immorality and bad conduct and oppression. He admonishes you that perhaps you will be reminded.*" Qur'an; 16:90). These elements are the pillars of the business approach in the Islamic context their corporate social responsibility basics.

Table 1 Approaches to corporate social responsibility from the Islamic perspective

Approach to corporate social responsibility	*Author(s)*
Tawhid paradigm	Muhamad (2007) and Muwazir et al. (2006)
Taqwa paradigm	Dusuki (2008)
Shariah's paradigm ("Maqasid al-Shariah") and the public interest (Mashalah)	Darrag and E-Bassiouny (2013), Darus et al. (2013), Dusuki and Abdullah (2007), Mohd Nor (2012), and Yusuf and Bahari (2011)
Ethical axioms (unity, equilibrium, free will, and responsibility)	Mohammed (2007)
Mandatory and recommended forms of Islamic CSR	Farook (2007)
Islamic economic responsibility, Islamic legal responsibility, Islamic ethical responsibility, Islamic philanthropic responsibility	Khurshid et al. (2014)
The application of public interest and importance of social capital	Yusuf and Bahari (2011)
Tawhid and Shariah paradigm should be integrated and discussed together	Abu Bakar and Yusof (2015)

Source Abu Bakar and Yusof (2015). Islamic concept of corporate social responsibility (CSR) from the perspective of CSR players at Bank Islam Malaysia Berhad and author

The aspect of understanding of corporate social responsibility in the Islam, quoted in Abu Bakar and Yusof (2015), in terms of conducted researches is given in Table 1.

From Table 1, we can see that most of the research was done in the period of the outbreak and after the global financial crisis. Generally, the main interest for Islamic economy started in the period after the crisis because Islamic approach to economy, economic matters, and society was seen as an example of how financial institutions should operate. This is important because in the period of crisis, the public lost trust in conventional financial system and trust is a result of a good implementation of corporate social responsibility which in the case of conventional financial system was missing.

3 CSR Based Projects—Some Cases from Banking Sector of Bosnia and Herzegovina

According to Central Bank of Bosnia and Herzegovina (Report on Financial Stability in 2016, 2017), there are 24 banks operating on the territory of B&H as follows: There are some identical banking brands mentioned several times, but they operate as independent legal entities mostly because of two entities—Federation of B&H and Republic of Srpska existing in Bosnia and Herzegovina with different banking laws.

All banks in Bosnia and Herzegovina have CSR aspects underlined on their websites and all the banks implement CSR mostly as charity activities. For example, Addiko bank donated 12.000 BAM to "Sveti Sava" primary school, and donated school furniture to "Ruđer Bošković" primary school in 2017. In 2016, Addiko donated 15.000 BAM to "Los Rosales" center for children with disabilities, and 15.000 BAM to "Prva osnovna škola" primary school in the same year. Addiko had more charity and donating activities mostly to schools and other educational institutions in previous years (Addiko Bank 2018). ASA Bank donated computer equipment to "Nafija Sarajlić" primary school in 2017 (ASA Banka 2017). Intesa Sanpaolo was undertaking "Inspired by Heart" campaign whereby 0.10 BAM was donated from every transaction made by Visa Inspire card users. Collected assets were donated to "Mirsad Prnjavorac" primary school in 2018, and other primary schools and hospitals in previous years (Intesa Sanpaolo 2018). ProCredit Bank was engaged in renovation of library in the faculty of economics in Sarajevo in 2017. ProCredit Bank undertakes credit line provided by the World Bank through the cooperation with OdRaz Foundation and the Federal Ministry of Finance. The credit line supports small and medium enterprises, and offers grace period from 12 months to 5 years in order to support development, stability, and sustainability of enterprises in the first period of business (Pro-Credit Bank 2017). The credit line is implemented by UniCredit Bank as well. In cooperation with USAID Guarantee Fund, UniCredit Bank offers the opportunity to finance investments in fixed assets, permanent craft, and working assets with coverage of 50% risk by Guarantee GF USAID. The USAID Guarantee Fund is operating in order to stimulate the development of the targeted sectors of the B&H economy: agricultural production, food production, wood processing, processing industry, tourism. Credit scale and condition varies from case to case with the maximum period of 36 months. UniCredit Bank undertakes another CSR based crediting in cooperation with the European Bank for Reconstruction and Development (EBRD) through the Program for Financial Support to Renewable Energy for the Western Balkans II (WeBSEFF II). The aim of the credit line is long-term financing of investment projects in renewable energy sources and energy efficiency that includes free technical assistance and non-refundable incentives for the European Union to support efforts to effectively use and conserve energy in the region (Unicredit Bank 2018).

Raiffeisen bank donated 2.500 BAM to "Home for the children without parents" in 2018 and was engaged in many activities as a sponsor in previous years. They provide special credit programs for small companies in B&H with 12 months grace period in cooperation with European Investment Bank (Raiffeisen Bank 2018). Sberbank BH gave a significant contribution in CSR activities in previous years. They donated a car to a humanitarian organization "Hilfswerk Austria International" in 2013. In the same year, they donated furniture to the "Center for Social Work" in Tešanj. From 2014 to 2017, they were engaged in donations to the hospital in Zenica, kindergarten in Zenica and Visoko, primary schools in Živinice and Gračanica, as well as other activities (Sberbank BH 2017). Sparkasse Bank organizes a public tender every year for sponsorship and donations in order to show transparency and justice. Usually they provide donations to schools, children centers, hospitals, and others (Sparkasse Bank 2018). Vakufska banka had donations toward "Parents house" in 2017 and 2018 (Vakufska banka 2018). Ziraat Bank gave significant contribution to CSR undertaking donation activities and financing programs in order to help B&H economy. They implement Turkish credit line (TCL/TFL) together with Bosna Bank International with the aim to support agriculture, production, and tourism in B&H. Assets are provided by T.C. Ziraat Bankasi A.S. Turkey.[2] TCL users are individuals and companies. There is possibility for 0.00% financing up to 50.00000 BAM. Beside TCL, Ziraat bank gave contribution to donating activities such as: donations to schools and student scholarships.

4 Islamic Banking and CSR in Bosnia and Herzegovina

First initiatives to establish a domestic bank that will operate according to Islamic law occurred in twentieth century at the beginning of 1990s. It was supposed to be the first Islamic bank in former Yugoslavia, established with intention to support development and to strengthen relations between Yugoslavia and Islamic Republic of Iran. The residence of the bank was planned to be in Sarajevo. The events that followed (war) stopped these pragmatic plans (Hadžić 2014). Enacting Islamic law principles to domestic banking system occurred in 1992 when Vakufska banka d.d. was established in Sarajevo. It was the first bank in Bosnia and Herzegovina that obliged itself to work according to Islamic law principles in volume that state law allows. Beside these plans and policies, today, Vakufska bank works as a conventional bank (Hadžić i Efendić, Development of Interest-free Banking in Bosnia and Herzegovina—Historical Aspects 2012). The first bank in Bosnia and Herzegovina that worked according to Islamic law in volume that state law allows was Orient bank d.d. in Sarajevo. This bank was offering non-interest credit services and bringing foreign investors in order to make its capital stronger. This bank was closed after the census of minimal needed capital for banks in Federation of B&H. After this, Orient bank was incorporated to the conventional ABS bank d.d. in Sarajevo (Štulanović and Hadžić 2007).

Nowadays, the only Islamic bank in B&H is Bosna Bank International (BBI). Bosna Bank International (BBI) d.d. Sarajevo was established in 2000. It was intended to work according to Islamic law and the banking legislature in B&H (Goksu and Becic 2012). The initial capital of BBI at that time was 47.5 million BAM, and authorized capital was 300 million USD. BBI founders were Islamic Development Bank 45.46%, Dubai

[2] *Source* https://www.bbi.ba/bs/pravna-lica/turska-kreditna-linija.

Islamic Bank 27.27%, and Abu Dhabi Islamic Bank 27.27% (Štulanović and Hadžić 2007).

When it comes to the CSR activities of BBI bank, it undertakes financing projects linked with CSR as follows: Turkish financing line (TFL), IDB Trust fund, and Al-Maktoum fund. All listed are socially responsible financing projects in order to support economy of B&H, agriculture, production, repatriate population, sustainable return of refugees, and displaced people more specifically. Beside CSR financings, BBI implements other CSR projects such as student scholarships, BBI Academy, BBI VIP Business Club, and other projects with the aim to connect clients and educate the population about Islamic banking and its principles (Bosna Bank International 2008, 2009, 2012).

5 The Use of Databases as a Scientific Tool

Databases can be defined as "*a set of data organized in a logical sequence that allows simple access, so that the information it contains can be: updated, used at any time by any computer program which it is connected to and operated at all times according to different criteria*" (Luque 1995). As a scientific tool, they can be used for the analysis of a certain number of articles, or other type of documents, as well as for the estimation of the number for different types of documents published in international referred journals in previous period. The growth of scientific researches that were collected in bibliographic databases has led to the use of "*bibliometrics*" as a useful tool to measure scientific activity based on the statistical analysis of quantitative data provided by scientific literature (Sancho 1990).

In that aspect, bibliometric analysis can be observed as a statistical analysis of written publications in order to provide a quantitative analysis of academic literature. Repanovici (2010) defines bibliometric as the "*application of mathematical and statistical methods to papers, books and other means of communication that are used in the analysis of science publications.*" Publication of research results for dissemination of scientific knowledge is a common scholarly practice (Shah et al. 2017).

As mentioned before, Scopus and WoS index base were used. Scopus was introduced by Elsevier in November 2004 and the name, Scopus, was inspired by the bird, Hammerkop (*Scopus umbretta*), which reportedly has excellent navigation skills (Burnham 2006). Scopus includes[3] over 71 billion records, 23.700 peer-reviewed journals, 1.4 billion cited references after 1970, 8.3 million conference papers, 300 trade publications and Articles-in-press and more than 166,000 books and 600 book series. According to Chadegani et al. (2013), most of the institutions in all over the world, including Latin America, Europe, North America, Australia, Asia, and the Middle East believe Scopus has positive influence on their researches.

On the other hand, WoS uses cited reference search to track prior research and monitor current developments in over 100 years' worth of content that is fully indexed, including 59 million records and back files dating back to 1898.[4] All this indicates that research done by using these databases can give a closer look at the level of development of a certain scientific area.

Authors Jacso (2005), Falagas et al. (2008), and Li et al. (2010) compared these databases and concluded that there is a difference among them, especially in specific disciplines covered by these databases. For instance, Mingers and Lipitakis (2010) found that Google Scholar had a better coverage than WoS in the field of business and economics disciplines. According to Haddow and Genoni (2010), Scopus produces slightly higher citation numbers than WoS and covers more journals.

6 Process and the Results of the Research

Islamic economy is not a new trend in economic history. Islamic financial system began to develop when the process of decolonization started and the first Islamic bank, Mit Ghamr Savings, was founded in 1963 in Egypt and followed the mode of German Savings Bank. Ever since, Islamic economy and its postulates are developing and have its own rules and postulates. One such part of it is corporate social responsibility. This is the subject that has been in field of interests for more than last 50 years. We almost know everything about the conventional perspective of the corporate social responsibility. But what about the Islamic approach to CSR? Is

[3] For more detailed information visit: https://www.elsevier.com/solutions/scopus.

[4] For more detailed information visit: http://wokinfo.com/?utm_source=false&utm_medium=false&utm_campaign=false.

it explored enough or not? Is this segment of Islamic economic history relevant for the researches to explore?

In this research, the analysis was performed by searching the literature related to corporate social responsibility from the Islamic aspect. The research was done by analyzing the period from 1990 to 2017. In order to get a better perspective about the level of development of CSR from the Islamic point, we didn't use programs for bibliometric analysis but a direct approach to the databases. For instance, one such program "*Publish and Perish*" can be a very useful tool but it has limitations on maximum

Document search
Documents

Searched terms:
"Corporate social responsibility and Islam"
"CSR and Islam"
„Islamic corporate social responsibility"
„Islamic CSR"
„Islamic business ethics"

Fields included
„All fields"
„Article title, abstract, keywords"
„Article title"

Limit
1990-2017

Document type
All

Acces type
All

Fig. 1 Islamic approach to corporate social responsibility research process in Scopus for the period 1990–2017

Table 2 Number of documents published in Scopus database by each searched term with "all fields" included and "all type of documents", in the period 1990–2017

Searched term	*Fields included*	*Type of documents*	*Number of published documents*
Corporate social responsibility and Islam	All fields included	All type of documents	2.434
CSR and Islam	All fields included	All type of documents	3.890
Islamic corporate social responsibility	All fields included	All type of documents	2.192
Islamic CSR	All fields included	All type of documents	1.092
Islamic business ethics	All fields included	All type of documents	6.232

Source Authors calculation based on Scopus database

200 results that data sources allowed which for this research is not considered to be statistically correct. Graphic solutions in the paper are done by using E–Views 9 program. Because the Scopus and WoS database have different approach to bibliometric research, we will present the results separately.

Scopus database allows wide perspective of a research which can be done by using the "Document search," "Authors search," "Affiliation search," and "Advanced search". In the aspect of fields included, the research can relate to "All fields" or specific: "Article Title, Abstract, Keywords", "First author", "Article title", "Keywords", "Affiliation," etc. Figure 1 illustrates the research process in Scopus done in this paper.

The results of our research that includes the data retrieved from Scopus databases are given in Table 2 and Graph 1.

Graph 2 presents the number of published documents in each searched category. It is interesting to note the increased number of published documents in this area after the global financial crisis in 2007, when the global interest in Islamic economy started.

Generally, using "*All fields*" in the search is probably too wide because we can have results that can include only one word, for instance "*social*" or "*Islamic*" and have results that may give not the real number of documents exploring the corporate social responsibility from Islamic perspective. While using "*All fields*" in the analysis, this was the case because the

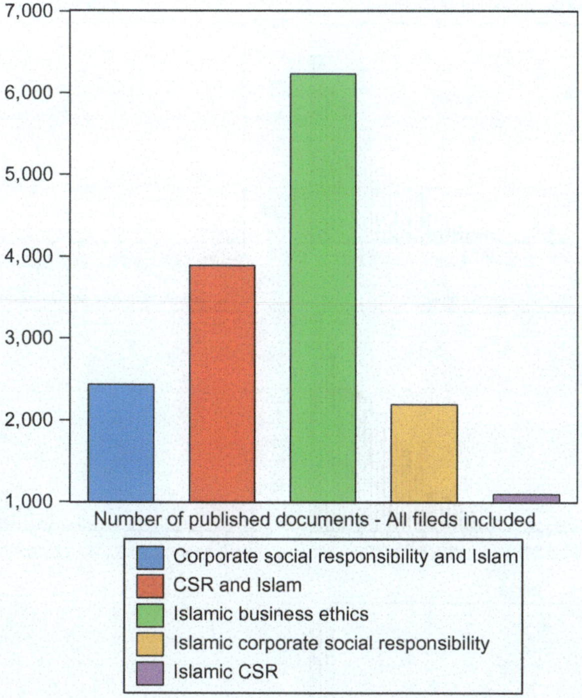

Graph 1 Searched terms with all documents and all fields included by the number of published documents in period 1990–2017

results included those terms were for instance, we have several institutions that are classified as dealing with Islamic economic taught (Graph 3).

If we use the synonym "CSR" instead of full title, the result will not be the same. It can be an issue because Scopus can in the analysis include, for instance, the name of the Journal that perhaps contains these letters like in our case where when defining the search term as "CSR" we got a result that included the name of Journal with that acronym (*Chemical Society Reviews*). *This may indicate a wrong conclusion on the actual number of published document in the field of corporate social responsibility. In our case the analysis showed that most of the documents in the area of "CSR and Islam" were published in China and by affiliations in China which is related to the issue mentioned above. This is presented in Graph 4 while in the previous this was the reason why we didn't include "CSR and Islam" in the analysis in the aspect of affiliation.*

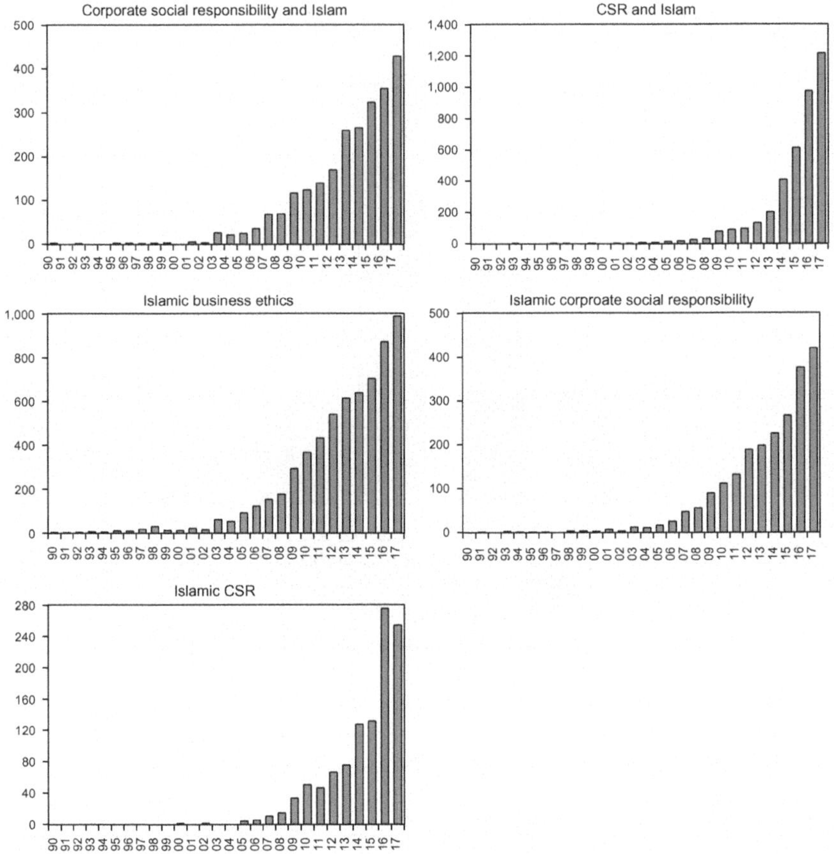

Graph 2 Searched terms with all documents and all fields included by the number of published documents for each year

In the previous part, we saw an analysis that included vide approach to the area of Islamic approach to corporate social responsibility. In the next part, we will analyze the number of published documents by using "*Article title, Abstract, Key Words*" for each of the mentioned terms. Because of this more specified approach, the number of published documents is significantly smaller than in the first case (Table 3 and Graph 5).

In Graph 6, we didn't include "Islamic business ethics" by affiliation because in this type of search it is important to notice that because of

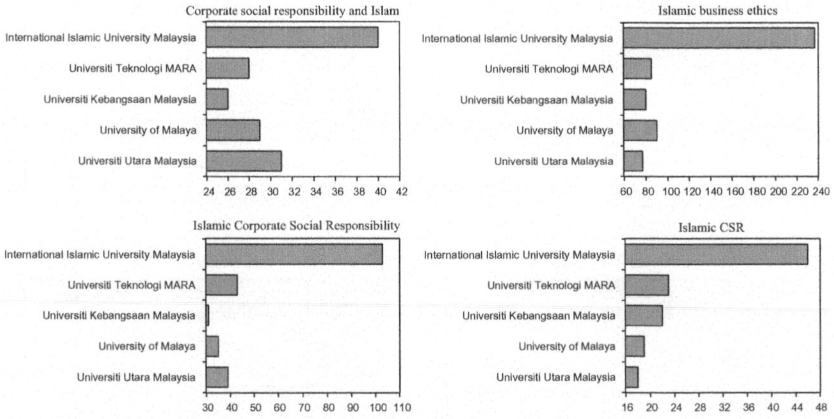

Graph 3 Searched terms with all documents and all fields included by the number of published documents—top 5 affiliations

the "Indexed keywords", Scopus can include documents, most of them, which are not part of the searched term like in our analysis regarding the term "Islamic business ethics" (Graph 7).

If we specify our search on "Article title" then we may have a better indicator about the number of published documents in the area of Islamic approach to corporate social responsibility (Table 4).

For instance, in the case of using "*Corporate social responsibility and Islam*" we found only one result—a book chapter titled "*Islam and corporate social responsibility in the Arab world: Reporting and discourse*" by Thibos and Gillespie (2011) published in "*Handbook of Islamic Marketing.*" In the field of using "*CSR and Islam*" the result is four documents as presented in Table 5.

In Islamic corporate social responsibility, we see an interest growing in this area especially in the period after the global financial crisis where the highest number of published documents was in 2014. It is interesting to note that the early documents that relate to the Islamic way of doing business is related to the Islamic business ethics, published in the 1999, as presented in Graph 8.

As seen from Graphs 8 and 9, most of the documents in the area of Islamic approach to corporate social responsibility were published in Malaysia and by authors employed in Malaysian academic institutions.

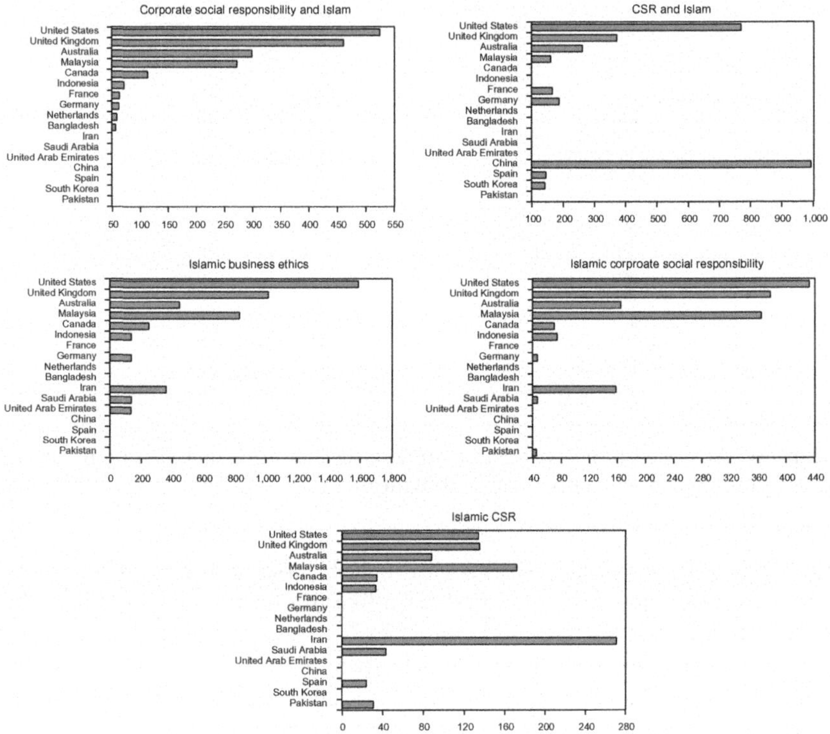

Graph 4 Searched terms with all documents and all fields included by the number of published documents by country

This is not surprise considering the fact that Malaysia is country number one regarding the Islamic Finance Development Indicator[5] (Thomson Reuters Report 2017). In religious aspect, the history of religious training in Malaysia goes back to the beginning of the thirteenth century which is connected with the arrival of Islam (Hashim and Langgulung 2008).

[5] Thomson Reuters Islamic Finance Development Indicator (IFDI) is consistent of 5 key dimensions that are important in the aspect global Islamic finance industry. IFDI includes: Quantitative Development (QD), Knowledge, Governance, Corporate Social Responsibility (CSR), and Awareness. For more visit: https://financial.thomsonreuters.com/en/markets-industries/islamic-finance.html.

Table 3 Number of documents published in Scopus database by each searched term with "Article title, Abstract, Key Words" included and "all type of documents", in the period 1990–2017

Searched term	*Fields included*	*Number of published documents*	*Type of documents*
Corporate social responsibility and Islam	"Article title, Abstract, Key Words"	43	All type of documents
CSR and Islam	"Article title, Abstract, Key Words"	32	All type of documents
Islamic corporate social responsibility	"Article title, Abstract, Key Words"	98	All type of documents
Islamic CSR	"Article title, Abstract, Key Words"	78	All type of documents
Islamic business ethics	"Article title, Abstract, Key Words"	218	All type of documents

Source Authors calculation based on Scopus database

Regarding the analysis we conducted, we conclude that Scopus gives a good perspective of published documents with the notice of more specifying the search term. In the aspect of using Web of Science database (WoS), we included only two fields of analysis: "Topic" and "Title." Using "Topic" as a search base is more widely and can generate data that are close to the searched terms, just like in the case of Scopus. The search results are given in Table 6.

Although we used "Topic" as a searched field, WoS shows significantly smaller number of published documents compared to Scopus. This is important to notice because in our search process we used "*All database*" that covers the search period from 1980. Graphs 10 and 11 show the number of published documents for each year and by country.

Like in the case of Scopus, regarding "Islamic business ethics" we note the writings in this area starts from 1999 while in the field of corporate social responsibility from 2000.

In order to specify the search, we used the "Title" as a searched field where the highest number of documents was published in the field of "Islamic corporate social responsibility".

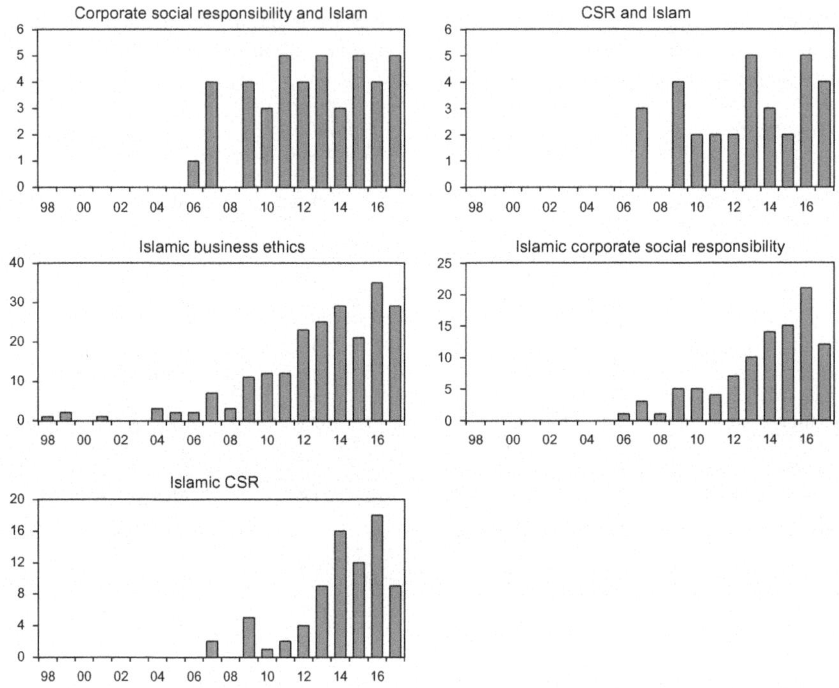

Graph 5 Searched terms with all documents and "Article title, Abstract, Key Words" included by the number of published documents for each year

The results in Table 7 indicate a lower number of published documents in terms of a specific search in WoS compared to Scopus.

7 Conclusions

Corporate social responsibility is a very active and important concept of modern business. It started its academic development in 1953 and it is still developing. It has been in field of interest for many researches and practitioners in every aspect of business activity. It has influence of company's image, financial activity, and performance. CSR has a wide range of literature in Western culture and business. In this paper, the focus was

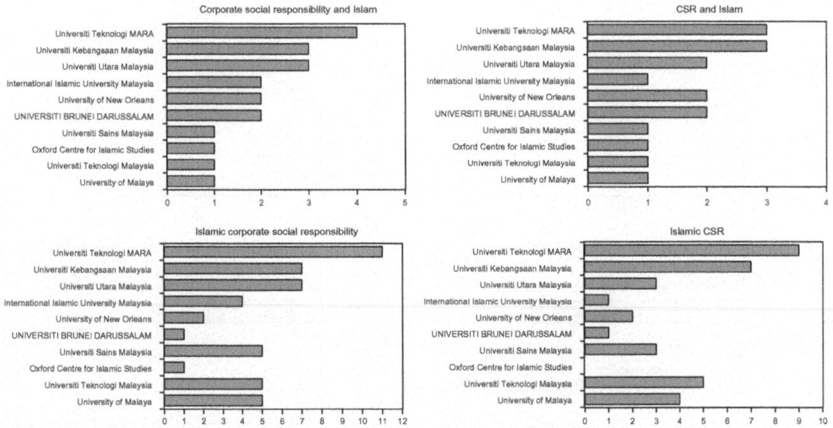

Graph 6 Searched terms with all documents and "Article title, Abstract, Key Words" included by the number of published documents by affiliation

placed on its academic development from the Islamic aspect and its presence in literature. In the process of research, two major databases were used; Scopus and WoS.

Regarding our first research question about the presence of the Islamic approach to corporate social responsibility in the research we can conclude that it is present but not on a sufficient level. More specified search shows that number from this field of economic taught should be higher. Causes of insufficient research in this area on a global scale could be that Islamic financial institutions and Islamic Scholars are observing corporate social responsibility as a part of Sharia and not as a separate entity. On the other hand, the reason could be that editors of high ranked Journals are considering Islamic economic taught still as the alternative way of doing business and are not giving it enough space for publishing.

When talking about the regions/countries in which this area of research is most present, this analysis shows that Malaysia is leading country. One of the reasons could be that this country has a long history and tradition in education, both comprehensible and religious. On the other hand, in the field of financial system, it has a dual banking system which gives a unique perspective for doing research and comparison between the conventional and Islamic approach to corporate social responsibility, in the field of banking.

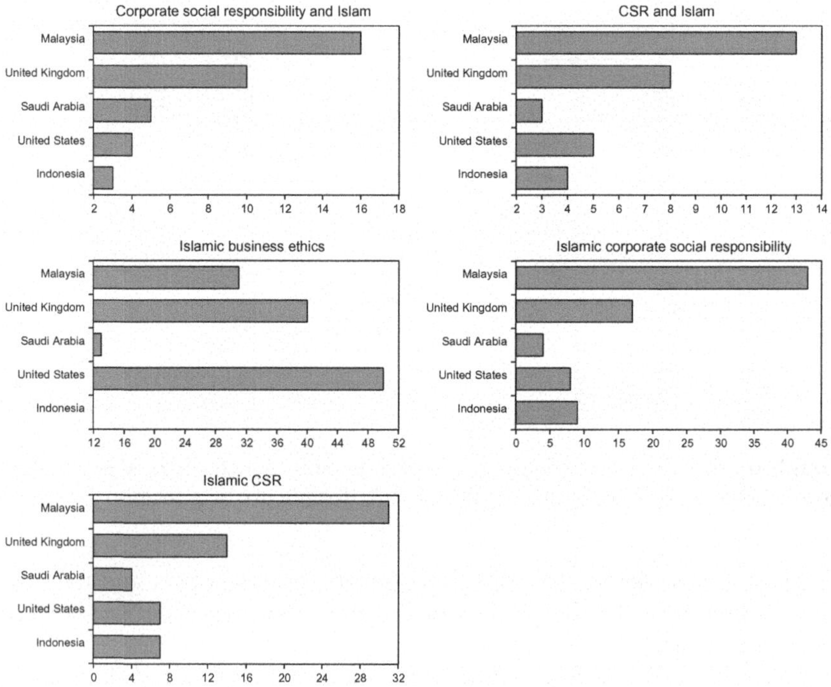

Graph 7 Searched terms with all documents and "Article title, Abstract, Key Words" included by the number of published documents by country

This research is a call for future students, researchers, and practitioners to involve more in the field of Islamic economy, ethics, and business. It can be associated with the education system where this area needs to be given additional attention and observed as a separate, special element which will certainly contribute to its further development.

From the research aspect, this paper has its own limitations. The process of research wasn't conducted with the use of a certain program for a bibliometric analysis. The number of published documents in this area is probably larger because many of the published articles or reviews from this field are not listed in Scopus or WoS. To get more precise results of research, more specific search needs to be conducted. Nevertheless, this research can make a contribution about the awareness of the number of documents published regarding the Islamic approach to corporate social responsibility and be a starting point for new research.

Table 4 Number of documents published in Scopus database by each searched term with "Article title" included and "all type of documents", in the period 1990–2017

Searched term	*Fields included*	*Number of published documents*	*Type of documents*
Corporate social responsibility and Islam	"Article title"	1	All type of documents
CSR and Islam	"Article title"	4	All type of documents
Islamic corporate social responsibility	"Article title"	40	All type of documents
Islamic CSR	"Article title"	11	All type of documents
Islamic business ethics	"Article title"	13	All type of documents

Source Authors calculation based on Scopus database

Table 5 Number of documents published in Scopus database using "CSR and Islam"

Searched term	*Name of the document*	*Author(s)*	*Year*
CSR and Islam	*Islam and CSR: A study of the compatibility between the tenets of Islam, the UN Global Compact and the development of social, human and natural capital*	Zinkin, J.	2007
CSR and Islam	*Islam and CSR: A study of the compatibility between the Tenets of Islam and the UN global compact*	Williams, G., Zinkin, J.	2010
CSR and Islam	*Managing CSR initiatives from the Islamic perspective: The case of Bank Islam Malaysia Berhad (BIMB)*	Bakar, F. A., Yusof, M. A. M.	2016
CSR and Islam	*Challenges in CSR engagements: The case of bank Islam*	Bakar, F. B. A., Md Yusof, M. A.	2016

Source Authors calculation based on Scopus database

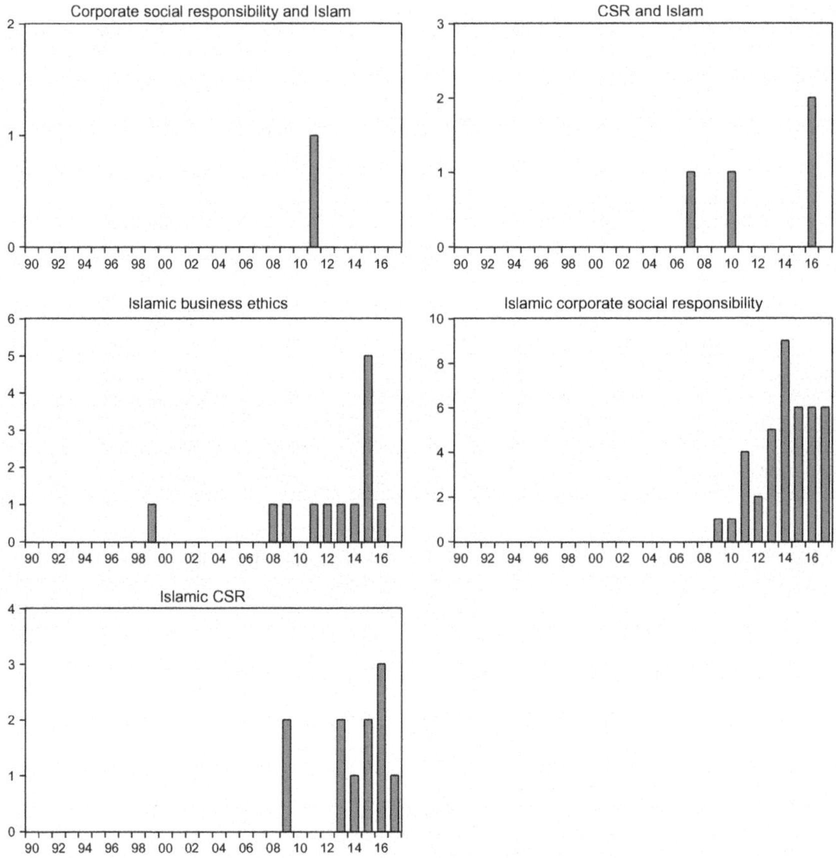

Graph 8 Searched terms with all documents and "Article title" included by the number of published documents for each year

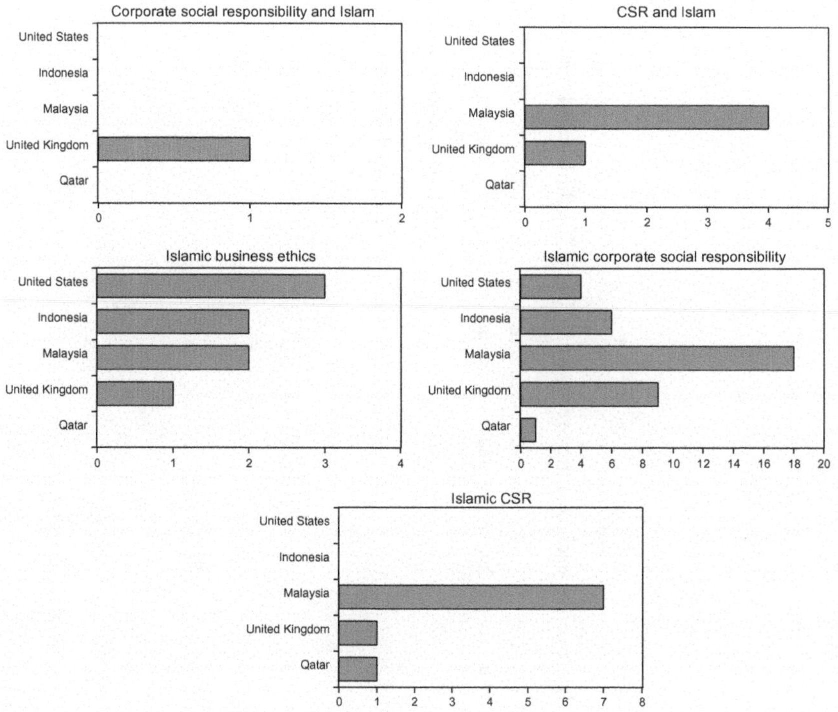

Graph 9 Searched terms with all documents and "Article title" included by the number of published documents by country (top 5)

Table 6 Number of documents published in WoS database by each searched term with "Topic" included and "all type of documents", in the period 1990–2017

Searched term	*Fields included*	*Number of published documents*	*Type of documents*
Corporate social responsibility and Islam	"Topic"	16	All type of documents
CSR and Islam	"Topic"	10	All type of documents
Islamic corporate social responsibility	"Topic"	64	All type of documents
Islamic CSR	"Topic"	38	All type of documents
Islamic business ethics	"Topic"	107	All type of documents

Source Authors calculation based on WoS database

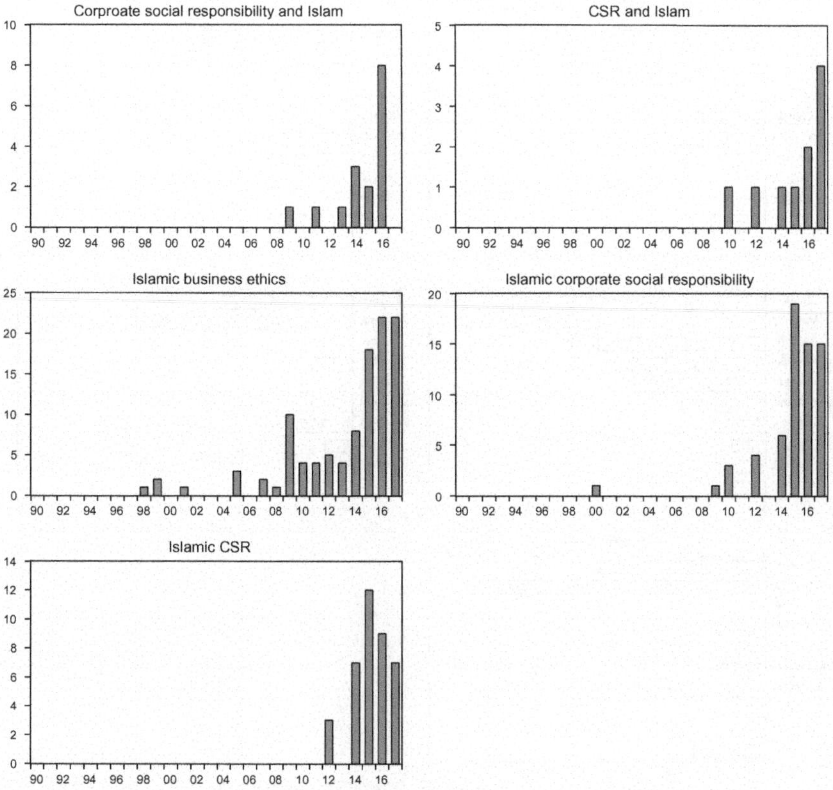

Graph 10 Searched terms with all documents and "Topic" included by the number of published documents for each year

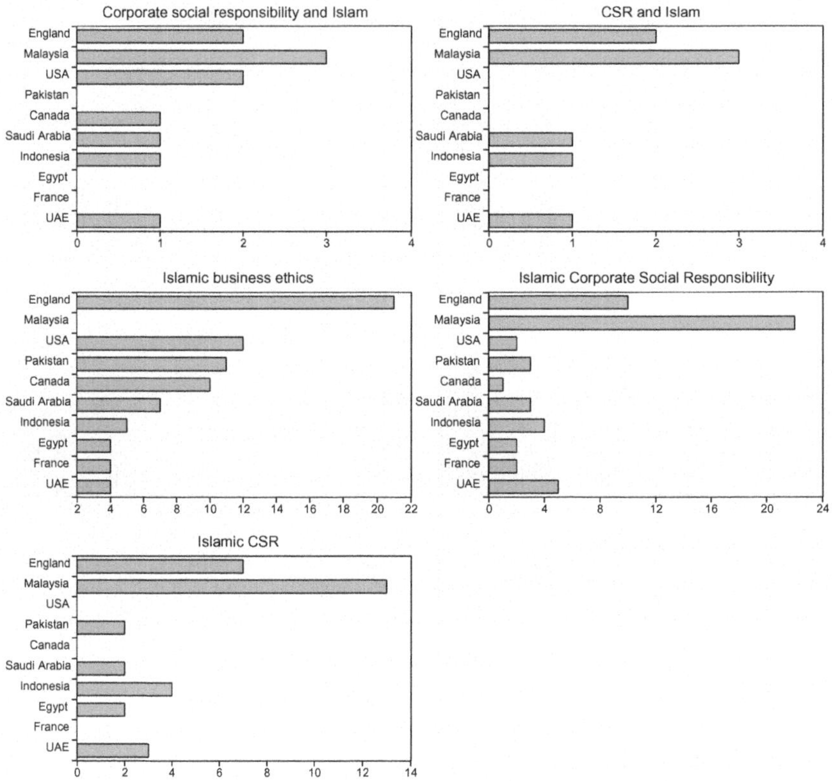

Graph 11 Searched terms with all documents and "Topic" included by the number of published documents by the country

Table 7 Number of documents published in WoS database by each searched term with "Title" included and "all type of documents", in the period 1990–2017

Searched term	*Fields included*	*Number of published documents*	*Type of documents*
Corporate social responsibility and Islam	"Title"	0	All type of documents
CSR and Islam	"Title"	1	All type of documents
Islamic corporate social responsibility	"Title"	12	All type of documents
Islamic CSR	"Title"	5	All type of documents
Islamic business ethics	"Title"	11	All type of documents

Source Authors calculation based on WoS database

References

Abu Bakar, F., and Yusof, M. A. M. (2015). *Islamic Concept of Corporate Social Responsibility (CSR) from the Perspective of CSR Players at Bank Islam Malaysia Berhad.* International Conference on Accounting Studies (ICAS), Johor Bahru, Johor, Malaysia.

Addiko bank d.d. Sarajevo. (2018). *Annual Report.*

ASA Banka. (2017). https://www.asabanka.ba/drustvena-odgovornost/.

Asutay, M. (2007). Conceptualisation of the second best solution in overcoming the social failure of Islamic banking and finance: Examining the overpowering of homoislamicus. *International Journal of Economics, Management*, 2(2), 167–195.

Auda, J. (2007). *Maqasid Al-Shariah as philosophy of Islamic Law: A Systems Approach.* The International Institute of Islamic Thought.

Badawi, J. A. (2001). Islamic Business Ethics. Retrieved from http://www.fiqhcouncil.org/node/17.

Beekun, R. I. (1996). *Islamic Busienss Ethics.* International Institute of Islamic Thought.

Beekun, R. I., and Badawi, J. A. (2005). Balancing ethical responsibility among multiple organizational stakeholders: The Islamic perspective. *Journal of Business Ethics*, 60(2), 131–145.

Bosna Bank International. (2008). *Annual Report.*

Bosna Bank International. (2009). *Annual Report.*

Bosna Bank International. (2012). *Annual Report.*

Bowen, H. R. (1953). *Social Responsibilities of Businessmen.* New York, NY: Harper & Row.

Brammer S., Millington, A., Rayton, B. (2007). The contribution of corporation social responsibility to organizational commitment. *International Journal of Human Resource Management*, 18(10), 1701–1719.

Burnham, J. F. (2006). Scopus database: A review. *Biomedical Digital Libraries*, 3(1). http://dx.doi.org/10.1186/1742-5581-3-1.

Carroll, A. B. (1979). A three-dimensional conceptual model of corporate performance. *Academy of Management Review* 4, 497–505.

Caroll, A. B. (1991). The pyramid of corporate social responsibility: Toward the moral management of organizational stakeholders. *Business Horizons*, 34(4), 39–48.

Carroll, A. B. (1999). Corporate social responsibility: Evolution of a definitional construct. *Business and Society*, 38, 3.

Centralna banka Bosne i Hercegovine. (2016). *Financial Stability Report.*

Centralna banka Bosne i Hercegovine. (2017). *Financial Stability Report.*

Chadegani, A. A., Salehi, H., Yunus, M. M., Farhadi, H., Fooladi, M., Farhadi, M., and Ebrahim, N. A. (2013). A comparison between two main academic

literature collections: Web of science and Scopus databases. *Asian Social Science*, 9(5), 18–26.
Dahlsrud, A. (2008). How corporate social responsibility is defined: An analysis of 37 definitions. *Corporate Social Responsibility and Environmental Management*, 15, 1–13. https://doi.org/10.1002/csr.132.
Darrag, M., and E-Bassiouny, N. (2013). An introspect into the Islamic roots of CSR in the Middle East: The case of Savola Group in Egypt. *Social Responsibility Journal*, 9(3), 362–378.
Darus, F., Yusoff, H., Abang Naim, D. M., Mohamed Zain, M., Amran, A., and Fauzi, H. (2013). Islamic Corporate Social Responsibility (i-CSR) framework from the perspective of Maqasid al-Syariah and Maslahah. *Issues in Social & Environmental Accounting*, 7(2), 102–112.
De George, R. T. (1982). *Business Ethics*. New York and London: Macmillan, Collier.
Dodd, E. M. (1932). For whom are corporate managers trustees? *Harvard Law Review*, 45(8), 1365–1372.
Dusuki, A. W. (2008). What does Islam say about corporate social responsibility (CSR)? *Review of Islamic Economics*, 12(1).
Dusuki, A. W., and Abdullah, N. I. (2007). Why do Malaysian customers patronise Islamic banks. *International Journal of Bank marketing*, 25(3), 142–160.
Ellegaard, O., and Wallin, J. A. (2015). The bibliometric analysis of scholarly production: How great is the impact? *Scientometrics*, 105, 1809–1831.
European Commission. (2011). Communication from the commission to the European Parliament, the Council, the European Economic and Social Committee and the Committee of the Regions. *A Renewed EU strategy 2011–14 for Corporate Social Responsibility*.
Falagas, M. E., Kouranos, V. D., Arencibia-Jorge, R., and Karageorgopoulos, D. E. (2008). Comparison of SCImago journal rank indicator with journal impact factor. *The FASEB Journal*, 22(8), 2623–2628. http://dx.doi.org/10.1096/fj.08-107938.
Farook, S. (2007). On corporate social responsibility of Islamic financial institutions. *Islamic Economic Studies*, 15(1), 31–46.
Frederick, W. C. (1998). Moving to CSR4. What to pack for the trip? *Business and Society*, 37(1), 40–59.
Frederick, W. C. (2006). *Corporation Be Good! The Story of Corporate Social Responsibility*. Indianapolis: Dog Ear Publishing.
Friedman, M. (1970). The social responsibility of business is to increase its profits. *New York Times Magazine*, p. 32.
Goel, M. D., and Ramanathan, E. P. (2014). Business ethics and corporate social responsibility—Is there a dividing line? *Procedia Economics and Finance*, 11.

Goksu, A., and Becic, A. (2012). Awareness of Islamic banking in Bosnia and Herzegovina. *International Research Journal of Finance and Economics*, 100, 1–14.

Guz, A. N., and Rushchitsky, J. J. (2009). Scopus: A system for the evaluation of scientific journals. *International Applied Mechanics*, 45(4), 351–362. http://dx.doi.org/10.1007/s10778-009-0189-4.

Haddow, G., and Genoni, P. (2010). Citation analysis and peer ranking of Australian social science journals. *Scientometrics*, 85(2), 471–487.

Hadžić, F. (2014). *Islamsko finansijsko tržište*. Sarajevo: Ekonomski fakultet.

Hadžić, F., and Efendić, V. (2012). *Development of Interest Free Banking in Bosnia and Herzegovina*. International Conference: Business in Between Cultures—The Development of Islamic Finance.

Hashim, C. N., and Langgulung, H. (2008). Islamic religious curriculum in Muslim countries: The experiences of Indonesia and Malaysia. *Bulletin of Education & Research*, 30(1), 1–19.

Hayat, U., and Malik, A. (2014). *Islamic Finance: Ethics, Concepts, Practice* (Literature Review). Available at http://www.cfapubs.org/doi/pdf/10.2470/rflr.v9.n3.1.

Iqbal, Z., and Mirakhor, A. (2011). *An Introduction to Islamic Finance*. http://doi.org/10.1002/9781118390474.ch8.

Intesa Sanpaolo. (2018). https://www.intesasanpaolobanka.ba/en/aktuelno.php?id=149.

Ismail, A. G., Zali, A., N. (2014). *Ethics in Relation to Islamic Finance Activities*. IRTI Working Paper Series, WP# 1435-07.

Jacso, P. (2005). As we may search—Comparison of major features of the Web of Science, Scopus, and Google Scholar citation-based and citation-enhanced databases. *Current Science*, 89(9), 1537–1547.

Jamali, D., and Sidani, Y. (2013). Does religiosity determine affinities to CSR? *Journal of Management, Spirituality & Religion*, 10(4).

Khurshid, M. A., Al-Aali, A., Soliman, A. A., and Mohamad Amin, S. (2014). Developing an Islamic corporate social responsibility model (ICSR). *Competitiveness Review*, 24(4), 258–274.

Kotler, P., and Lee, N. (2005). *Corporate Social Responsibility: Doing the Most Good for Your Company and Your Cause*. Hoboken, NJ: Wiley.

Krooss, H. B. (1970). *Executive Opinion: What Business Leaders Said and Thought on Economic Issues 1920s–1960s*. New York, NY and Garden City: Doubleday & Co.

Lenk, H. (1996). *Ethik in der Wirtschaft*. Stuttgart: Verlag W. Kohlhammer

Li, J., Burnham, J. F., Lemley, T., & Britton, R. M. (2010). Citation analysis: Comparison of Web of Science, Scopus, SciFinder, and Google Scholar. *Journal of Electronic Resources in Medical Libraries*, 7(3), 196–217. http://dx.doi.org/10.1080/15424065.2010.505518.

Luque, T. (1995). Líneas de investigación y bases de datos para la investigación. *Investigaciones Europeas de Dirección y Economía de la Empresa*, 1(2), 35–50.
Mayhew, L. H. (Ed.). (1982). *Talcott Parsons: On Institutions and Social Evolution*. Chicago, IL: University of Chicago Press.
Mingers, J., and Lipitakis, E. (2010). Counting the citations: A comparison of Web of Science and Google Scholar in the field of business and management. *Scientometrics*, 85(2), 613–625.
Mohammed, J. A. (2007). *Corporate Social Responsibility in Islam*. PhD dissertation.
Mohd Nor, S. (2012). Integrating moral in a dynamic model of corporate social responsibility in Islamic economics and finance. *Asian and African Area Studies*, 11(2), 137–150.
Muwazir, M., Muhamad, R., and Noordin, K. (2006). Corporate social responsibility disclosure: A Tawhidic approach. *Journal of Syariah*, 14(1), 125–142.
Naqvi, S. N. H. (1981). *Ethics and Economics—An Islamic Synthesis*. Leicester: The Islamic Foundation.
Naqvi, S. N. H. (2003). *Perspectives on Morality and Human Well-Being: A Contribution to Islamic Economics*. Leicester: The Islamic Foundation.
Nasution, M. E. (2009). Islamic spirit and morale in economics. *Journal of International Development and Cooperation*, 15(1–2), 113–124.
ProCredit Bank. (2017). https://www.procreditbank.ba/novost/12/procredit-bank-i-efsa-uprilicili-svecanu-primopredaju-uredenog-bibliotecko-informacionog-centra.
Raiffeisen Bank. (2018). https://raiffeisenbank.ba/en/node/2039.
Ramasamy, B., Yeung, M., and Au, A. (2010). Consumer support for corporate social responsibility (CSR): The role of religion and values. *Journal of Business Ethics*, 91, 61–72.
Repanovici, A. (2010). Measuring the visibility of the university's scientific production through scientometric methods an exploratory study at the Transylvania University of Brasov, Romania. *Performance Measurement and Metrics*, 12(2), 106–117. https://doi.org/10.1108/14678041111149345.
Sancho, R. (1990). Indicadores bibliométricos utilizados en la evaluación de la ciencia y la tecnología. *Revisión bibliográfica Revista Española de Documentación Científica*, 13(3–4), 842–863.
Sberbank BH. (2017). *Godišnji izvještaj*.
Shah, S. R. U., Mahmood, K., and Dean, A. H. (2017). Review of Google scholar, Web of Science, and Scopus search results: The case of inclusive education research.
Sharani, U. M. (2004). *Corporate Social Responsibility Underlines Values Propagated by Islam*. Bernama: Kuala Lumpur.
Sparkasse Bank. (2018). https://www.sparkasse.ba/bs/o-nama/drustveno-odgovorno-poslovanje.

Štulanović, M., and Hadžić, F. (2007). *Osnovi islamske ekonomije i financija*. Islamski Pedagoški fakultet u Bihaću.

Thibos, C., and Gillespie, K. (2011). Islam and Corporate Social Responsibility in the Arab World: Reporting and Discourse. In *Handbook of Islamic Marketing* (pp. 300–318). Edward Elgar Publishing Ltd.

Thomson Reuters. (2017). *Islamic Finance Development Report*.

Unicredit Bank. (2018). https://www.unicredit.ba/ba/korporativni_klijenti/finansiranje/kreditne_linije.html.

Usmani, M. T. (2002). An introduction to Islamic finance Arab and Islamic Law and their harmonization in Islamic banking and finance. In *Islamic Finance*.

Vakufska banka. (2018). www.givingbalkans.com.

Votaw, D. (1973). Genius Becomes Rare. In *The Corporate Dilemma*. Edited by D. Votaw and S. P. Sethi. Englewood Cliffs, NJ: Prentice Hall.

Yusuf, M. Y., and Bahari, Z. (2011). *Islamic corporate social responsibility in Islamic banking: Towards poverty alleviation*. Paper presented at the 8th International Conference on Islamic Economics & Finance, Doha, Qatar.

CHAPTER 4

Potentials of Waqfs from a Socio-Economic Perspective: The Case of Bosnia and Herzegovina

Velid Efendic and Mensud Bisić

Key Topics

- Waqf and endowments,
- The role of waqfs in economic development,
- Socio-economic perspective of waqfs,
- History of waqf developments in Bosnia and Herzegovina,
- Current issues and challenges in waqf management.

V. Efendic (✉) · M. Bisić
School of Economics and Business,
University of Sarajevo, Sarajevo, Bosnia and Herzegovina
e-mail: velid.efendic@efsa.unsa.ba

V. Efendic (ed.), *Islamic Finance Practices*,
https://doi.org/10.1007/978-3-030-34420-7_4

1 Introduction

The survival of the *waqf*s for greatly longer than half of millennium is remarkable and shows the endurance of the system (Cizakca 1998). These charitable foundations, which were established within the Islamic civilization across the Islamic world, were also introduced in Bosnian society five centuries ago. As a part of the institutional framework of Islamic economics, it played a major role in the development of urban public space in Bosnia during the Ottoman period, and hence, it represented the footing for cities establishment.

All over the country, the wealthy Muslim people, inspired by a desire to support the poor members of the civil society, and all activities, which people can benefit from at large, through an organized and sustainable system, established a huge number of facilities such as schools, mosques, hospitals, roads, bridges and water supply systems that successfully contributed to the welfare of the community (Hoexter 2002). However, despite the overwhelming achievements, and significant contribution that this institution made in the socio-economic development of the Bosnian state during the Ottoman period, it experienced the dramatic decline and neglect in the post-Ottoman period. Unfortunately, even now, *waqf* institution has not been recognized as a system that can significantly contribute towards the expectation of Islamic economy.

The rigid interpretation of the traditional *waqf* regulations, traditional methods of *waqf* management and the classical system of *waqf* prevented *waqf* from giving an adequate response to the requirements of modern societies. Therefore, the *waqf*s should undergo serious reconstruction and reorient their missions, in order to be attached to the current socio-economic development (Boudjellal 2005). To implement this, it is essential to explore today's awareness of *waqf*s socio-economic potential amongst the members of the Islamic Community (IC), policymakers and other relevant players. It is also crucial to evaluate the status of *waqf* institutions in B&H in relation to their substantial aspirations (maqasid al-shari'ah—promotion of human well-being) and sustainability as both provide the rationale for their existence in the current structure. This will help to locate how the *waqf*s institutions are managed in the utilization of the allocated assets, and help in establishing a new productive and efficient system for *waqf*s management in B&H that meets the expectations of Islamic economic and management standards.

After the war in B&H ended in 1995, the government struggle to enhance the country's economic growth and development. Accordingly, the alternatives that could help in building a sustainable bridge across this gap would be very beneficial for country's development. The third sector, as one of the alternatives, is getting recognized in B&H in recent times, in the overall economic growth and welfare programs. Muslims of B&H (50% of the population[1]) can contribute to such efforts by promoting appropriate institutional settings such as *waqf*. The institution of *waqf*, as a model of social entrepreneurship, with a new system redesigned in accordance with the modern socio-economic perspective, can play a significant role and apply to the given parameters of the practical reality of B&H.

The above-mentioned method provides a strong justification for a detailed theoretical and empirical study of the potential of *waqf* system to be employed as a remarkable contributor to the economic growth and social welfare, in B&H and wider.

This research aims at exploring the potential of *waqf* institution in B&H to sustain a balanced economic development, support social needs and services, and hence improve the social welfare of the community. At the first place, the current performance of *waqf*'s institutions in B&H will be evaluated. The crucial factors that caused the decline of *waqf*'s institution will be critically reviewed and the reasons for why this typical Islamic heritage nowadays does not play an exceptionally important role in the development of the settlements in providing funds for public facilities will be addressed. In addition, perceptions of sampled members of IC have been evaluated in relation to the understanding of *waqf* and its historical role as well as their readiness for the new endowments for socio-economic development.

Additionally, further analysis of perceptions and understanding of *waqf* system within the members of IC of B&H will be explored, in order to identify the right steps for modernization and development of existing *waqf*s and encourage the establishment of new models of *waqf* according to modern needs such as cash *waqf*.

The paper is organized as follows: Sect. 2 provides the literature review of waqfs. Section 3 presents the background of waqfs in B&H, Sect. 4

[1] Agency for statistics in Bosnia and Herzegovina, Census of population, households and dwellings in Bosnia and Herzegovina, 2013, final results: http://www.popis.gov.ba/popis2013/knjige.php?id=2.

covers the methodology and data, Sect. 5 presents the empirical results, while Sect. 6 provides conclusions with policy recommendations.

2 Literature on Waqfs

Most of the scholars define and understand *waqf* similarly while their interpretation of the *waqf's* essentials defers slightly. Al Sarkhasi (1978) states that *waqf* means to hold specific property and preserve it for the confined benefit of a certain benevolence, prohibiting any use or disposition of it outside of that particular objective. According to (Al Abadi 2001), Hanafi scholars defined *waqf* as an exclusion of an asset from a waqif's property and dedication of its revenue or benefits to charitable, pious cause. However, the most concise definition, based on the Prophet's (p.b.u.h.[2]) sayings, states that *waqf* is the preservation of an asset and its utilization for the charitable objectives.

When it comes to the economic perspective of the waqf, it can be defined as switching funds and other assets from spending, and investing them in creative properties that supply either usufruct or revenues for future consumption by individuals or group of individuals (Pirates and Abdolmaleki 2007). As a part of the voluntary sector, *waqf* provides certain welfare-enhancing services to the society by financing them through the investment of the allocated resources. *Waqf* is an action that involves investment for the future and accumulation of productive wealth that benefits future generations (Kahf 1998). It is a philanthropic organization that aims to supply future generations with income and social services through sacrificing contemporary consumption opportunities (Kahf 1998). Besides, it is an endowment with high power that moves the society towards growth and prosperity (Yalawae and Tahir 2003).

Although it was not mentioned directly in the Quran, its basic concept was: "By no means shall ye attain righteousness unless ye give (freely) of that which ye love; and whatever ye give, of a truth *Allah* knoweth it well" (*Quran*, Chapter *Ali Imran*, 92). According to Bukhari and Muslim, the Prophet (p.b.u.h.), referred to this verse saying: "When the son of Adam dies, all his deeds come to an end, except for three: ongoing charity, beneficial knowledge or a righteous son who will pray for him". Referring to this, Cizakca (1998) stated that Muslim society needed such

[2] Peace be upon Him.

a mechanism that would enable them to perform all three good deeds together.

However, the first ever *waqf* in the history of Islam was founded by the very Prophet (p.b.u.h.), upon his arrival from Makkah to Madinah. Prophet (p.b.u.h.) built the first ever mosque in the history of Islam, founding, in this way, also the first ever *waqf* in the history of Islam. Modified Quba mosque stands even now, at the same place (Kahf 2003). Since that time, this system has been embraced so enthusiastically by the Islamic civilization and developed to such a unique dimension.

When it comes to the classification of waqfs, according to Kahf (2003), there are two basic types of *waqf* s—public and private *waqf. Waqfs* established to serve the social needs and well-being of the society in all, like public utilities, education, healthcare, libraries, the poor and the needy, are called public philanthropic *waqfs* (Kahf 2003, p. 2). Mosques and facilities confined to secure the revenues to cover the expenses related to the mosques are in the category of the public religious *waqf* s. This sort of *waqf* is essential to the society as it serves various spiritual needs and thus decrees the cost of religious activities for the future generations (Kahf 2003, p. 2). However, the *waqfs*, in which the offspring of the founders are the primary recipients of their revenues, are known as private family *waqfs* or *waqfahli*. This means that public benefit, in this case, was not the priority.

There was another type of *waqf*, established in fifteenth century in the Ottoman Empire—the cash *waqf* (Cizakca 2000). This *waqf* was providing service to human beings in the name of Allah. Social services such as health and education in the Ottoman economy were fully supplied by gifts and endowments (Cizakca 2000, p. 45). Therefore, the cash *waqf* played a vital role in the Ottoman financial system and was incredibly popular during the sixteenth century in the Ottoman Empire.

The purpose of *waqf* is to arrange and manage the state of richness and wealth in the Islamic society in order to drive the society towards development and success. Cajee (2008) reports that eventually, *waqf* becomes a powerful community supporting institution, e.g. provision of infrastructure and social services such as health and educational programmes.

Islamic economic system strives to eradicate the poverty, establish socio-economic justice and distribute income justly to achieve human well-being. These are some of the primary goals of Islam and thus should be unyielding features of an Islamic economic system (Chapra 1992). According to Khan (1997), *adl* (social justice) and *Ihsan* (benevolence) are the fundamental axioms of Islamic economic system. This concept implies the existence of mechanisms and instruments that would assist in taking care of those who cannot be taken care of by the market, who cannot play with economic forces or who do not have access to financial means to enable them to exploit the commercial opportunities around them.

Waqf also influenced the development of urbanization and civilization greatly. A system called *imaret*, established and managed by *waqf*, comprised of a combination of various facilities, typically, in Ottoman Empire, has played a considerable role in the establishment and development of Turkish and Muslim cities, and generally in the social and economic life of the country (Cem 2003). Roadhouses and arcades, bakeries, mills, workshops, bazaars, butcheries, marketplaces, food houses, guesthouses (*tabhane*), hospitals (*darussifa*), baths (*hammam*), caravansaries and residences of the officers and employees of these institutions, as well as infrastructure facilities and various buildings dependent on them, generally located around an educational or religious institution such as a mosque, a madrasah, or a library, as a *waqf* focal point, comprised the skeleton of the new city or district to be built or an old city (Cem 2003).

According to Batuta (2001), *waqf* institution in Damascus was utilized for various and peculiar purposes to achieve harmony life for human society, such as *waqf* for performing pilgrimage to Makkah, *waqf* for contributing to marriage or tie knot, *waqf* for free of offence, *waqf* for the food, *waqf* for the cloth and *waqf* for upgrading the infrastructure such as road facilities.

Although there is a significant development of waqfs in B&H, there are no many studies that explored socio-economic role of waqfs in B&H. However, there are some resources and records on waqfs in B&H that confirm the significance of this institution for country's development.

3 Background on Waqfs in Bosnia and Herzegovina

Carrying the main burden of the religious, educational and social welfare of Muslims in the post-Ottoman time, *waqf* has become inherent in their daily lives. Also, through the process of endowment, Bosnian Muslims were able to achieve social reputation and prestige as well (Hadžic 2014). However, due to the dramatic history of Bosnian state, this institution has survived unfavourable stages, experiencing a great destruction of its properties (Hadžić and Efendić 2012).

The origin of *waqf* institution in Bosnia dates from the first arrival of Islam on its land around 500 years ago. It was the time of the great conquests of the Ottoman Empire. In the summer 1463 Ottoman army conquered Bosnia. It was probably the first contact between Bosnia and Islam (Malcom 1994).

Upon the arrival of Ottoman Empire, Bosnia had become a part of a new social and political system. More than 80% of the cities in present Bosnia had been built by the end of sixteenth century on the *waqf* basis (Malcom 1994), which is visible even in their very names: *Donji Waqf, Skender Waqf, Kulen Waqf Varcar Waqf* (Krkic 1989).

Sarajevo has witnessed a rapid development in the seventeenth century to the extent that was regarded as one of the wonders of Balkans, and undoubtedly one of the most important inland cities (Malcom 1994).

Although waqfs had reached their successful development and culmination in the Ottoman Empire, they have been experiencing a serious decline, neglect and destruction, starting from the nineteenth century, as a result of dramatic historical and political circumstances. According to Cizakca (1998), these turbulent downs were connected to the politics of the states under which they existed. After Austria-Hungary occupied B&H in 1878, according to the provisions of the international law, the occupation implied the retention of the status quo, maintaining the existing legal order in B&H. Based on these facts, Austria-Hungary was obliged to accept the already established state of affairs even in the case of *waqf*s administration and management (Karcic 1983). As consequences of the new situation, bureaucratic functionaries were highly paid at the expense of *waqf* beneficiaries: schools, mosques, needy, etc. (Karcic 2009). In addition, besides the usurpation of the many waqfs, Austro-Hungarian government used *waqf* funds to build 145 facilities, hotels, houses and cafes (Donia 1981) which were not aligned with the waqifs' wills.

After Austro-Hungarians, the new governor of B&H came on scene, the Kingdom of Serbs, Croats and Slaves (KSCS, from 1918 until 1939) that was placed in Southeast Europe and Central Europe consisting of today's Serbia, Montenegro, Kosovo, Vojvodina, Croatia, B&H and Slovenia. During this period, many *waqfs* have been devastated, alienated and demolished. The new dictatorship, along with the passed regulation, enabled the regime to appoint the main bodies of this united IC and control the administration and the management of the *waqf* properties (Durmisevic 2011). However, Belahija (1933) argues that besides these questionable circumstances, *waqf*s, already abandoned, have become agitated means of reckless individuals willing to sacrifice everything for their success. Not only in poor financial management, but especially in the unwise conduct of religious, educational policy, *waqf*s and consequently, the whole IC experienced one of their worst periods.

After KSCS, the new communist system of SFRY (Socialist Federal Republic of Yugoslavia) wanted to eliminate the influence of any religion considering it a barrier standing on the path to the unification of all Yugoslav nations and the establishment of the new political order Durmisevic (2011). Conducted by these principles, the communists have brought a series of measures and laws that have produced a considerable damage to all religious communities, but especially to the IC of B&H and its waqf properties. Through the nationalization of 1946, 1948 and 1958, the dominant state ownership was realized in all economic sectors including real estate as well. According to the report, prepared by the Commission for Religious Affairs of B&H from September 1961, 803 objects of IC in B&H were nationalized, which represented 53.7% of the total IC's objects before nationalization. As, by 1961, the total number of nationalized religious objects reached 992, of which 80.9% belonged to the IC of B&H, it was evident that the IC was the largest victim and loser, and probably the target, in the process of nationalization of religious properties (Muderis 2013).

The modern history of B&H was started since its independence in 1992. According to (Omerdic 1999) during the war in B&H that took place from 1992 to 1995, 1347 waqf objects were destroyed: 614 mosques, 218 masjids, 69 maktabs, 4 tekkes, 37 turbeh and 405 other different waqfs. Within this period, IC in B&H showed a determination to fight for the restitution of seized waqf property, to protect and improve existing waqfs, but also to provide conditions for new endowment and its further development, primarily by revival of the Waqf Directorate, 37 years after it was shut down (Muderis 2013).

Waqf Directorate (WD) has undertaken a vast number of activities related to the development and implementation of various projects aimed at improving the work of the WD, reconstruction and revitalization of the waqf facilities, development, and improvement of waqf institution in B&H and encouragement and promotion of new endowment (Muderis 2013).

During the process of waqf registration, WD has recognized eight general existing categories of waqfs: religious objects (4563 unit), lands (9500 units), residential facilities (1610), public areas such as parks, streets, gardens, bridges (1928 units), business facilities (892), educational institutions (26), commercial facilities like stores and shops (599), and utilities (28).

Since its re-establishment, WD noted growth in the number of *endowments*. So far 271 real estate objects have been endowed, 2641 cash waqf and 420 certificate waqfs (Zaimovic 2013). However, the presented statistical data do not treat the real value of the waqfs endowed.

After the periods of stagnation, caused mainly by the usurpation of the vast number of waqf properties and lousy management of the IC members, the institution of *waqf* has shown signs of the promising revival.

4 Methodology and Data

This research benefits from primary data collected through questionnaire surveys. The questionnaires were distributed amongst the Islamic Community of Bosnia and Herzegovina focusing on the various mosques in the area. The study aimed to collect data from 250 questionnaires and capture a representative portion of the local population, based on both age and gender, amongst other factors. The questionnaires comprised 34 questions, assessing demographic information, such as age and profession, with further questions relating to the population's awareness of the *waqf* concept alongside other information relevant to the case study.

The questionnaire was distributed manually over two weeks, in mosques, community centres, "women's" groups and door to door. It was hoped that by distributing the questionnaire in such a way, a broader cross-section of respondents would be achieved, while also ensuring a high response rate. The return rate was 90% for the 250 questionnaires returned, in a way conducive to analysis. The questionnaire was composed in the Bosnian language and was left with respondents in order to provide more time to seek assistance in completing it. This resulted in the non-completion of some questionnaires and is the prominent reason for a reduction in the response rate.

The questionnaire was divided into five sections. The first two sections focused on personal information and institutional belongings and acted as the control variable from which further analysis is conducted. The following three sections of the questionnaire focus on crucial aspects of the overall research study: awareness of *waqf*, principles of *waqf*, perceptions of *waqf*, interest in the new *waqf* and, finally, the socio-economic impact of *waqfs*.

For the second stage of the analysis, quantitative methods of descriptive statistical methods and inferential statistics, Kruskal–Wallis test (KW test) and the Mann–Whitney U test (MWU test) are implemented in order to identify the understanding of *waqf* system by members of IC.

5 Empirical Findings

This section portrays the demographic profile of the respondents, detailing information such as age, profession, educational achievement and membership of the IC and whether they are waqifs (donors). The detailed information is shown in Table 1.

As detailed in Table 1, the majority of the sampled participants were female, with a frequency of 54.1%, whereas male participation was slightly less with a frequency of 45.1%. This is a small difference, so it can be concluded that the survey is equally balanced between two genders. Hence, results imply that there is no gender bias within Bosnian Muslim society.

Additionally, the majority of the participants were in the 31–40 age group, representing 50.2% of the age demographics and thus emphasizing the youthful composition of the society. On the whole, respondents' age varied between the range of 31 and 60 years, which is considered to be the prime working age, collectively representing 70.1%. As this research is attempting to assess, in part, the awareness of Bosnian Muslims concerning *waqf*, it is encouraging to record such a high ratio of the respondents within this age group.

Educational level of the correspondents is of the specific interest. The Islamic finance and economics sector often criticizes a lack of awareness amongst the broader population of the basic details of Islamic finance and economy and its internal operations. The research recorded 51.1% of respondents stating that they have academic qualifications at undergraduate level, 11.1% reported Masters' level, while Ph.D. and specialization respondents represent 3.3%. The mean average of the findings is 4.3909 meaning that the median value complies with the educational levels of high school and undergraduate qualifications.

In terms of the participants' employment, the respondents who work constitute 58%, whereas those unemployed total 11.4%, despite a high unemployment rate in B&H. As a large number of the respondents stated

Table 1 Results for the respondents profile

Response categories					
		Frequency	*Percent*	*Mean value*	*Standard deviation*
(Q1) Gender					
Valid	Male	110	45.1	1.5455	0.49896
	Female	132	54.1		
	Total	242	100		
(Q2) Age					
Valid	Up to 30 years	67	27.6	2.0082	0.8479
	From 31 to 40	122	50.2		
	From 41 to 50	43	17.7		
	From 51 to 60	7	2.9		
	Above 61	4	1.6		
	Total	243	100		
(Q3) Education status					
Valid	Elementary school	0	0	4.3909	1.65627
	Primary school	65	26.7		
	Secondary school	4	1.6		
	College	13	5.3		
	Graduate	126	51.9		
	Specialist	5	2.1		
	Master	27	11.1		
	PhD	3	1.2		
	Total	243	100		
(Q4) Employment status					
Valid	Employed	158	58	1.9136	1.39537
	Honorary/seasonal worker	9	5.7		
	Unemployed	43	11.4		
	Pensioner	5	1.4		
	Other	28	25.7		
	Total	243	100		

that they had academic qualifications at undergraduate level, in addition to the youthful composition of the participants, it may be presumed that a significant number of the participants, defining their profession as other, were in fact students. Moreover, a significant number of the respondents, 25.7%, fitted the category who do not have regular employment.

5.1 *Institutional Belonging*

This section, which is summarized in Table 2, assesses the participants' awareness of institutional belonging in regard to the Islamic Community and endowing the *waqf*. 76.2% of respondents stated that they are a member of the Islamic Community which presents a high level of belonging to the Muslim community in B&H. However, amongst them, only 57.3% are practising religious obligations in mosques regularly. On the other hand, the vast majority of the participants in the survey stated that they are not *waqifs*, 66.4%. This discrepancy between institutional belonging and *waqf* endowments points to an essential fact that the majority of participants do not understand the meaning of *waqf*. This is because the majority of the members of the Muslim community gives money to establish new mosques, graveyards, Islamic schools, etc., but they did not count them as a *waqf* endowment.

Although the vast majority of respondents stated that they are not *waqifs*, the majority of the respondents indicated that the money they gave for benefits of the Islamic Community, 90.6%, is a type of *waqf*. This further indicates a different understanding of *waqf* amongst the community members.

In addition, 42.7% of participants stated that someone from their family donated a *waqf*, which indicates that senior family members are much more prone to finance an endowment—65.6% of grandparents and 26.0% of parents. Only 4.1% of participants amongst the younger generation are *waqifs*. This implies that *waqf* awareness amongst the working educated class is shallow in the Bosnian community. This response is supported by the mean value of 1.5208 and the standard deviation value of 0.94009.

5.2 *Perception of Waqf*

This part of the questionnaire (Table 3) is focused on the Islamic jurisprudential elements of *waqf*, concentrating on the notion of who can be *waqif*, what can be *waqf*, the will of donor, distribution and repossession of *waqf*s. The questions in this section are focused on general principles relating to historical and jurisprudential issues regarding *waqf*.

Having received a response rate of 76.2%, as seen in Table 2, stating institutional belonging to the Muslim community in B&H, that coupled with the fact that Muslims can only be *waqf*, 48.0%, is a crucial tenet of *waqf* because it is a religious act. However, some respondents stated that

Table 2 Summary results for the questions Q5–Q10

		Frequency	*Percent*	*Mean value*	*Standard deviation*
(Q5) Are you a member of the Islamic Community?					
Valid	Yes	182	76.2		
	No	57	23.8	1.2385	0.42706
	Total	239	100		
(Q6) How often do you come to the mosque?					
Valid	Several times a week	134	57.3		
	Once a week	33	14.1		
	Once a month	31	13.2	1.8803	1.17311
	Only during Ramadan	33	14.1		
	Only on the Eid prayer	3	1.3		
	Total	234	100		
(Q7) Are you *waqif* (donor)?					
Valid	Yes	81	33.6	1.6639	0.47336
	No	160	66.4		
	Total	241	100		
(Q8) If yes (if your answer on the previous was yes) what have you donated?					
Valid	Land	2	2.4	3.8471	0.54567
	Facility (house, store etc.)	1	1.2		
	Mosque	5	5.9		
	Money for *waqf* development	77	90.6		
	Other	0	0		
	Total	85	100		
(Q9) Did someone from your family donated a *waqf* (endowed)?					
Valid	Yes	103	42.7	2.1079	1.0901
	No	37	15.4		
	I am not sure	73	30.3		
	I do not know	28	11.6		
	Total	241	100		
(Q10) If you have answered the question 'Yes', which member of your family endowed? (You can choose more responses)					
Valid	Grandmother/grandfather	63	65.6	1.5208	0.94009
	Father/mother	25	26		
	Brother/sister	3	3.1		
	Son/daughter	1	1		
	Other relatives	4	4.2		
	Total	96	100		

Table 3 Summary results for the questions Q11–Q15

		Frequency	*Percent*	*Mean value*	*Standard deviation*
(Q11) Who can be waqif					
Valid	All people of all faith	93	38.9	2.056	1.44434
	Only Muslims	117	48		
	Only members of the Islamic Community	4	1.7		
	I do not know	25	10.5		
	Total	239	100		
(Q12) *Waqf* is donated exclusively for religious purposes?					
Valid	Strongly agree	42	17.4	3.1074	1.29987
	Agree	37	15.3		
	Do not know	45	18.6		
	Disagree	89	36.8		
	Strongly disagree	29	12		
	Total	242	100		
(Q13) *Waqf* is given for purposes that may be used by non-Muslim as well?					
Valid	Strongly agree	74	30.7	2.1079	0.97723
	Agree	92	38.2		
	Do not know	54	22.4		
	Disagree	17	7.1		
	Strongly disagree	4	1.7		
	Total	241	100		
(Q14) It is necessary to execute waqif's will if such exist?					
Valid	Strongly agree	94	39	1.9502	0.94737
	Agree	82	34		
	Do not know	51	21.2		
	Disagree	11	4.6		
	Strongly disagree	3	1.2		
	Total	241	100		
(Q15) *Waqf* can be sold seized or abused?					
Valid	Strongly agree	8	3.3	4.2551	1.0045
	Agree	4	1.6		
	Do not know	39	16		
	Disagree	59	24.3		
	Strongly disagree	133	54.7		
	Total	243	100		

38.9% of all religious people can be *waqif* which further confirms the misunderstanding of the central principle of *waqf*. This shallow awareness of *waqf* is supported by the fact that 18.0% of respondents stated that they did not know what *waqf* was used for and 32.7% of those expressed that the *waqf* was only used for religious purposes. The mean value of 3.1074 placed the average response within the category of familiarity and a low standard deviation value of 1.12987, meaning that those responses express no or little familiarity with the term of *waqf*.

However, when the participants were asked, whether *waqf* can be used for non-Muslims, 68.9% stated that it could. Hence, there are contradicting results from the previous question.

Finally, the participants were asked about their familiarity with the *waqif's* will and whether a *waqf* can be sold or seized. Only a small number of respondents (14 participants) stated that a *waqif's* will could be changed, while 73% of respondents noted that the *waqif's* will has to be respected. Perhaps surprisingly, 4.9% of the respondents stated that the *waqf* could be sold or seized. The mean value indicates that the majority of respondents were not familiar with basic *waqf* rules. However, the standard deviation between 0.94737 and 1.4434 mean values shows that there was indeed a significantly wide spectrum of answers, which effectively emphasizes the general lack of knowledge in terms of the Islamic rules and practices connected to the *waqf*.

Table 4 assesses the Islamic Community members' perceptions of *waqf* regarding its role in civil society and the benefits that are expected. When asked about whether *waqf* can be returned to a *waqif*, 53.3% of participants either agreed strongly or agreed that it is not allowed to return a *waqf*. However, the striking figure is the ratio of the respondents who were undecided—29.6%, as to whether or not this was the case. The mean value was 2.4417 which locates the average response between the categories of agree and undecided which is aligned with the percentages stated here. As to the question that addressed the issues of importance of *waqf* in civil society, the most common response was that of "strongly agree", comprising 67.8% of respondents. In regard to the question of benefits of *waqf*, most of the respondents believe that *waqf* benefits "people and the Islamic community". The mean value for the question was between 2.6337 meaning that the majority of responses perceived *waqf* as mainly beneficial for Islamic Community and people in general. Finally, when the respondents were asked about *waqf*'s benefits in this world and the hereafter, 86.4% gave a positive answer. In short, we may conclude that the

Table 4 Summary results for the questions Q16–Q19

		Frequency	*Percent*	*Mean value*	*Standard deviation*
(Q16) *Waqf* cannot be returned to *waqif*?					
Valid	Strongly agree	59	24.6	2.4417	1.1337
	Agree	69	28.7		
	Do not know	71	29.6		
	Disagree	29	12.1		
	Strongly disagree	12	5		
	Total	240	100		
(Q17) *Waqf* is an important institution for the promotion of the welfare of the society?					
Valid	Strongly agree	164	67.8	1.3595	0.55309
	Agree	69	28.5		
	Do not know	9	3.7		
	Disagree	0	0		
	Strongly disagree	0	0		
	Total	242	100		
(Q18) In your opinion, who benefit from the *waqf*?					
Valid	People	38	15.6	2.6337	0.75625
	Islamic Community	16	6.6		
	Both people and Islamic Community	186	76.5		
	I do not know	3	1.2		
	Total	243	100		
(Q19) *Waqf* does not bring benefits in the hereafter, *waqf* exclusively grants benefits on this world?					
Valid	Strongly agree	6	2.5	4.405	0.92972
	Agree	6	2.5		
	Do not know	21	8.7		
	Disagree	60	24.8		
	Strongly disagree	149	61.6		
	Total	242	100		

general awareness of *waqf's* socio-economic potential amongst the Muslim community is very good.

5.3 Role of the Muslim Community in Creating Awareness About Waqf

This section of the analysis focuses on the role of the IC in creating awareness about *waqf*. However, as the knowledge of principles of *waqf* amongst the participants was diverse, this section also aimed to assess the general impute to engage the community members in creating awareness about *waqf*, whether as a beneficiary or as a donor. When asked from where do community members obtain information about *waqf*, most of the participants 28.1% mentioned Friday sermons and 21.5% religious books. However, a significant number 22.1% stated that they do not have enough information about *waqf*, while 60% of respondents reported that they are undecided whether local imams engage in talking about *waqf*s and engaging the community. The community also suggested that the best tool for promoting *waqf* should be the Islamic newspaper (Preporod), 48.1%. Therefore, we can conclude that the Islamic Community should utilize better available tools, such as the newspaper and the Friday sermons in creating awareness about *waqf* in Bosnian society (Table 5).

5.4 A Motivation for *Waqf* Endowments

The following section of this analysis aims to assess the motivation for endowments and the creation of new *waqf*s in response to the contemporary needs. When asking participants as to their reasons for attaining endowments, most participants stated that they are looking for reward in the hereafter, 43.0%. In addition, 43% stated that they are looking for reward both in this world and in the hereafter. When the participants were asked for the explicit reasons for endowments, 21.4% of responses stated "local community", followed by 14.6% of Muslims in general. The lowest number was given to Mufti district, 2.4%, as they are reluctant to support *waqf*s whose benefit goes to a limited group of beneficiaries (Table 6).

When asked what the reasons (Table 7) that they have not undertaken endowments until now are, the responses stated 64.9% citing they are not sufficiently wealthy. This can be explained by the economic situation in Bosnia due to the war which caused the massive destruction to public and private sectors. 10.6% of respondents mentioned that they are not familiar with the concept of *waqf*, while 6.0% expressed dissatisfaction with the Islamic Community in B&H's management of *waqf*. The mean value in response to the questions addressing this subject was 2.2025 and 1.7381, which, when taking into the account the value of standard deviation, can be interpreted as the community's lack of financial means for contributing to new *waqf* establishments.

The community members' motivation for an endowment is a fundamental principle behind this survey. Therefore, it is favourable to see that

Table 5 Summary results for the questions Q20–Q22

		Frequency	*Percent*	*Mean value*	*Standard deviation*
(Q20) I learned sufficient information about *waqf* from (you can choose more than one answer)					
Valid	Friday sermons and preaches	68	28.1	4.9174	2.74077
	Radio BIR	6	2.5		
	Islamic newspaper (*Preporod*)	4	1.7		
	The *Waqf* Directorate	8	3.3		
	The Islamic Community website	8	3.3		
	Religious books	52	21.5		
	I do not have enough information on *waqfs*	54	22.3		
	Other	42	17.4		
	Total	242	100		
(Q21) The *waqf* institution has given enough space and time for discussion in masjids?					
Valid	Strongly agree	12	1.4	3.2033	0.93772
	Agree	30	25.7		
	Undecided	116	60		
	Disagree	63	10		
	Strongly disagree	20	2.9		
	Total	241	100		
(Q22) The best promotion tool for *waqf* is (you can mark one or more responses)					
Valid	Radio	12	5	3.2033	0.93772
	Online sources	30	12.4		
	Islamic newspaper (*Preporod*)	116	48.1		
	Friday sermons and preaches	63	26.1		
	Special promotion of waqfs	20	8.3		
	Religious books	0	0		
	Other	0	0		
	Total	241	100		

Table 6 Summary results for the questions Q23 and Q24

		Frequency	*Percent*	*Mean value*	*Standard deviation*
(Q23) Only for *waqifs* (Please choose one or more answers)					
Valid	I endowed exclusively on purpose to gain an award in this world and *akhirah*	34	43	2.2025	1.14779
	I endowed exclusively in order to gain award on this world	0	0		
	I endowed exclusively in order to gain an award in the hereafter	43	54.4		
	I endowed to gain reputation	1	1.3		
	I endowed to get *waqufiyyah* certificate	0	0		
	It is important to have my name on the endowed facility	0	0		
	I endowed because I have enough money	1	1.3		
	Total	79	100		
(Q24) The reason for endowment is to help					
Valid	Muslims	36	14.6	1.7381	2.12908
	Local Community	18	21.4		
	Majlis	7	8.3		
	Mufty district	2	2.4		
	State B&H	4	4.8		
	Islamic Community	10	11.9		
	Other	7	8.3		
	Total	84	100		

83.3% of participants said that they are happy that they have endowed. Only one participant stated that he/she is not satisfied with the endowment. The only reason for such feeling is related to the politeness of *waqf* management in the process of funding—30.8% "strongly agreed

Table 7 Summary results for the question Q25

		Frequency	*Percent*	*mean value*	*Standard deviation*
(Q25) (Only for those who did not endow) Mark one or more of the answers: I did not obscure because of the following reasons					
Valid	I am not sufficiently wealthy	98	64.9	2.649	2.41716
	I want to leave my belongings to my children / wife / family	5	3.3		
	I do not think that it is important to support Islamic Community through the institution of *waqf*;	0	0		
	I believe that it is more important to give up your property for charitable purposes (the needy)	1	0.7		
	I am not familiar enough with the *waqf's* institution	16	10.6		
	I am not satisfied with the performance of the Islamic Community	9	6		
	Other	22	14.6		
	Total	93 or 38%	100		

and agree" with the statement. However, 31.9% answered with uncertainty as the majority of participants did not have experience of going through procedures of endowment registration since their contribution to *waqf* was through cash. In regard to the conditions of *waqf*, 75.4% agreed that their will was respected. However, the small number of participants 7.8% expressed dissatisfaction. The reason for this dissatisfaction may be linked to the misunderstanding between donors and the management of *waqf* within the Islamic Community. The question of appreciation by the Islamic Community was received with uncertainty for the majority of participants, 38.5%. Also, there are 14.3% of participants who believe that the Islamic Community does not appreciate their contributions (Table 8).

In the further analysis of motivation for endowment (Table 9), the participants were asked what they have endowed. 75.0% of respondents stated that they had endowed money which is usually for building a mosque or a school and buying land for a graveyard. This result has been further supported with the question what is the most appropriate way for endowment, as the responses were fixed assets, 54.5%, and *sergiya*, 12.5%, which represent money. These figures somewhat summarize the overall

Table 8 Summary results for the questions Q26–Q29

		Frequency	*Percent*	*Mean value*	*Standard deviation*
(Q26) I'm happy to have endowed					
Valid	Strongly agree	80	83.3	1.25	0.64889
	Agree	10	10.4		
	Do not know	5	5.2		
	Disagree	0	0		
	Strongly disagree	1	1		
	Total	96	100		
(Q27) The WD management was kind and professional to me					
Valid	Strongly agree	28	30.8	2.1319	0.9799
	Agree	30	33		
	Do not know	29	31.9		
	Disagree	1	1.1		
	Strongly disagree	3	3.3		
	Total	91	100		
(Q28) All the conditions of my endowment are respected					
Valid	Strongly agree	33	38.8	1.8706	0.8134
	Agree	31	36.5		
	Do not know	20	23.5		
	Disagree	1	1.2		
	Strongly disagree	6	6.6		
	Total	91	100		
(Q29) The Islamic Community in B&H appreciates my contribution					
Valid	Strongly agree	15	16.5	2.5741	1.06607
	Agree	28	30.8		
	Do not know	35	38.5		
	Disagree	7	7.7		
	Strongly disagree	6	6.6		
	Total	91	100		

Table 9 Summary results for the questions Q30–Q32

		Frequency	*Percent*	*Standard deviation*
(Q30) I have endowed				
Valid	Building (mosque, *tekke, makteb, masjid,* other: house, apartment)	7	7.6	0.94086
	Land: agricultural land, road	4	4.3	
	Fountain	7	7.6	
	Money for a defined or undefined purpose	69	75	
	Other movable assets (vehicle, mosque equipment)	5	5.4	
	Total	92	100	
(Q31) I consider that the most suitable/easiest way to endow				
Valid	Donating immovable assets	109	54.5	2.16607
	Online donation	19	9.5	
	Bank transfer	14	7	
	Sergiya	25	12.5	
	Donor dinner	12	6	
	Movable assets (building materials, services, preparation of preliminary design, etc.	2	1	
	Other	19	9.5	
	Total	200	100	
(Q32) *Waqf* institution has a great potential to become a respectful tool for the realization of the social justice and equality				
Valid	Strongly agree	74	35.4	0.96728
	Agree	66	31.6	
	Do not know	60	28.7	
	Disagree	4	1.9	
	Strongly disagree	5	2.4	
	Total	209	100	
(Q33) *Waqf* can play an important role in the economic development of B&H, as it can cover those sectors not sufficiently covered, or not covered at all by the state				
Valid	Strongly agree	73	34.3	0.90186
	Agree	92	43.2	
	Do not know	39	18.3	
	Disagree	4	1.9	
	Strongly disagree	5	2.3	
	Total	213	100	

understanding of *waqf* concept within the Bosnian community which is presented in the three above-mentioned factors. Eventually, it can be concluded that the findings presented here indicate that the majority of the participants are not inflexible when it comes to the possibility of usage of *waqf* for different purposes, as was the case in the past. However, the participants currently suffer from a lack of knowledge and awareness.

The potential of *waqf* to become a working mechanism for wealth distribution and the establishment of social justice was positively received, 67%. Although 28.7% of participants were not sure, only 4.3% of the participants expressed their disagreement with this statement. Correspondingly, the answer related to the economic role of *waqf* in rebuilding B&H received a positive response: 77.5% of the respondents agree that this would be a positive step, while 18.3% are undecided. The reason for this indecision may be linked to the general lack of awareness of *waqf*, but also because the *waqf* is commonly used for philanthropic purposes and rarely for economic development.

Finally, Table 10 aims to assess the participants' opinion in terms of the transparency of the IC when it comes to the distribution and expenses of *waqf* funds, as a factor that can strongly influence their willingness to endow. The respondents' negative response of 27.3% was due to lack of

Table 10 Summary results for the questions Q34–Q35

		Frequency	*Percent*	*Mean value*	*Standard deviation*
(Q34) The Islamic Community of B&H transparently reports its members and potential *waqfis* on the and distribution and expenses of *waqf* funds					
Valid	Strongly agree	5	2.4	3.2392	0.95585
	Agree	29	13.9		
	Do not know	118	56.5		
	Disagree	25	12		
	Strongly disagree	32	15.3		
	Total	244	100		
(Q35) Islamic Community in Bosnia and Herzegovina has a clear vision and strategy on the development of *waqfs* in B&H					
Valid	Strongly agree	6	2.8	3.1934	0.94661
	Agree	30	14.2		
	Do not know	123	58		
	Disagree	23	10.8		
	Strongly disagree	32	14.2		
	Total	212	100		

disclosure in managing *waqf*s. 56.5% of participants were undecided on the statement which raises the issue of transparency within the existing *waqf* system. Perhaps, the main reason behind the lack of *waqf* donations is hidden in the existing management style, led by non-professionals in the field of management, economics and finance.

When participants were asked about a clear strategy in developing the new *waqf*s, 58.0% of responses stated "undecided", whereas only 17% of respondents expressed that there is a clear strategy for *waqf* enhancement. This negative vision regarding the future of *waqf* can only be explained by the presumption that the Islamic Community has done little to create awareness of *waqf* in terms of its appropriate use.

Therefore, it may be concluded that the results presented above suggest that the majority of respondents are willing to engage in *waqf* projects, build new *waqf*s or actively engage with the Islamic Community at large. Yet, the participants currently suffer from a lack of knowledge, awareness and distrust, due to a perhaps passive role adopted by the WDand the IC in creating awareness of *waqf* and its potential.

5.5 Second Stage Analysis

The previous section presented the descriptive analysis and made a good base for further investigation of the same data set, through cross-referencing the control categories, such as gender, education, age, employment, membership of the IC and previous engagement in the *waqf* projects with the variable questions. In an attempt to analyse the data set, searching for the statistically significant differences that may have arisen, the Kruskal–Wallis test has been employed.

The table in Appendix shows no statistically significant difference existing within the control category of employment if cross-referenced with questions in Appendix. However, it has been discerned that gender effects when the participants attend the mosque, with a p-value of 0.00. Besides, the data show noticeable differences in mosque attendance amongst the male category. It is clear that there is no considerable difference when cross-analysing the control category of gender amongst the remaining questions in Appendix.

The age category is significant in questions 6, 12 and 14 when cross-referenced with p-values of 0.007, 0.020 and 0.047, showing a clear difference and going up to 30 within the three questions. There are apparent differences in understanding the principles of *waqf* amongst the younger participants. The remaining questions are not significant in cross-referencing with age variables. In relation to the education variable, however, there is an observation of importance, noted when analysing the benefits of *waqf* in this world and the hereafter. According to the Kruskal–Wallis test, the Masters and Doctoral graduates are more familiar with the issue of *waqf* benefits and have an active knowledge of Islamic jurisprudence linked to *waqf* and *waqf* principles. The p-value recorded in this record is very low at 0.03, while the median scores for Ph.D. and Masters graduates' fields mainly attract attention, recording values of 168.00 and 147.50, respectively. The remaining questions are not significant in cross-referencing with the education variable. In the table in Appendix, the question centred on the mosque attendance has been significant for both variables—member of the Islamic Community and *waqif* with p-values of 0.014 and 0.000. This implies that being a member, or not, of the Islamic Community, as well as being a *waqif*, or not, has great importance in understanding the *waqf* concept. There were considerable statistical differences found across all control categories of "Yes", yielding a mean ranking of 121.96 and 128.98. Observed of further significance is the member of the Islamic Community in question 12 with a p-value of 0.041. There is also a statistically outstanding range of understanding related to questions 16 and 17, in accordance with being *waqif* or not, showing p-values of 0.005 and 0.002. The median value of 127.97 for the *waqif* group "No" shows that they had a noticeably different perception in comparison with the rest of the sample who opted for "Yes". Likewise, we can see that there is an impact of being a *waqif* in relation to the answers given regarding the potential of *waqf* to contribute to community development, as those who did not endow had a different understanding, registering a median value of 128.44. However, we can see that both control variables did not record any significances in the remaining questions in Appendix.

The control categories in response to remaining questions from the sample were cross-referenced and analysed in Appendix. There were no remarkable differences across the control categories of age, employment and membership of the IC. However, questions 28, 32 and 33, as expected, due to their nature, when cross-referenced with the control category of being a *waqif*, recorded some statistical differences, with p-values of 0.005, 0.005 and 0.004, respectively. Therefore, the impact that being or not being *waqif* has on the perception and understanding of the respondents in terms of *waqf* potential in establishing social justice and development in society can be discerned. Also observable is practical experience being more critical in implementing the values of Islam, such as *waqf* than theoretical knowledge. Question 34 identified a statistical difference concerning the strategy and the vision related to the future of *waqf*s in B&H with a registered p-value of 0.005 when considering educational levels. Moreover, and interestingly, gender also influenced the answers documented in regard to question 21, with a p-value of 0.006 and a median value 130.91 recorded amongst the female group, suggesting that female respondents are more concerned for *waqf* in the Bosnian community. The participant's responses to remaining questions are not significant within the categories.

Finally, we can conclude that the Kruskal Wallis analysis shows that the majority of the respondents are aware of the importance of *waqf* and its role in the socio-economic development of a society. However, it is noticeable that there is a significant lack of knowledge and awareness amongst the respondents in terms of *waqf* principles as practised and applied in Islamic law. Only those respondents with higher education appear to have any serious understanding of the *waqf*-related principles. Throughout the analysis, the impact that being an Islamic Community member and *waqif* had on the survey is significant. These control categories recorded more statistical differences than any other. However, oppositely, the control categories of education and employment had a minimal influence on the responses given. Conclusively, despite some misunderstanding of *waqf* principles and lack of motivation for new endowments and the vision for its development, it appears that the majority of respondents, especially *waqifs* and the members of an Islamic Community, are still greatly supportive of *waqfs* and the role it can play in increasing social justice and development.

6 Conclusions

The research confirmed that the waqfs in B&H had given a significant contribution to the socio-economic development of the Bosnian society. For the many generations, this instrument was successfully employed to combat poverty and enhance welfare. It provided material infrastructure and created a source of revenue that were utilized for various philanthropic, social, cultural and urbanization projects. Whole cities in B&H were built on the ground of waqf system. Waqf has not served only the Islamic Community. It also gave a significant contribution to the enhancement of the socio-economic, cultural and urban development of other religious groups in B&H, such as Christians and Jews that built their religious and other facilities, such as monasteries, churches and synagogues around these waqfs, thus proving that it can be used to build bridges between people of different religious background and serve as an alternative approach to solving contemporary socio-economic hardships in B&H and wider.

The study finds that a lack of awareness of waqf principles influenced waqf development negatively. However, this was not the main reason for the waqf decline in B&H. The majority of respondents, specially waqifs and the members of the IC, are still of great support for waqf and its role that it can play in increasing the social justice and development.

The study ascertains that, despite some signs of revival, this institution is still far from the utilization of its full potential. For its full revitalization and integration in economic development and poverty reduction and more dominant role in the enhancement of the socio-economic welfare, it has to be restructured and aligned with the contemporary needs and conditions.

Finally, our results reveal that majority of the respondents are aware of the importance of *waqf* and its role in the socio-economic development of a society. However, it is noticeable that there is a significant lack of knowledge and awareness amongst the respondents in terms of *waqf* principles as practised and applied in Islamic law. Only those respondents with higher education appear to have any serious understanding of the *waqf*-related principles.

Conclusively, despite some misunderstanding of *waqf* principles and lack of motivation for new endowments and the vision for its development, it appears that the majority of respondents, especially *waqifs* and the members of an Islamic Community, are still greatly supportive of *waqfs* and the role it can play in increasing social justice and development.

Appendix: Results of the Second Stage Analysis

Question	Gender	Mean rank	Asymp. sig	Age	Mean rank	Asymp.sig	Education	Mean rank	Asymp. sig	Employment	Mean rank	Asymp.sig	Member of IC	Mean rank	Asymp.sig	Waqif	Mean rank	Asymp.sig
(Q6) How often do you come to the mosque?							Elementary school	131.2										
				Up to 30	137.75		Primary school	67.5		Employed	109.77							
	Male	86.71		31to 40	114.7		Secondary school	91.69		Honorary	144.5		Yes	110.22		Yes	87.86	
	Female	144.09	.000*	41to 50	93.9	.007*	College	115.2	0.076	Unemployed	135.12	0.09	No	133.13	.014*	No	131.58	.000*
				51to 60	109.64		Specialist	146.13		Pensioner	125.25							
				61+	125.25		Masters	116.37		Other	122.96							
							PhD	67.5										
(Q12) *Waqf* is donated exclusively for religious purposes?							Elementary school	109.24										
				Up to 30	125.09		Primary school	108.5		Employed	120.73							
	Male	112.54		31to 40	126.61		Secondary school	87.88		Honorary	116.78		Yes	114.56		Yes	111.58	
	Female	127.99	0.076	41to 50	107.11	0.384	College	129.28	0.085	Unemployed	118.13	0.364	No	114.96	.041*	No	124.96	0.145
				51to 60	100.71		Specialist	151.3		Pensioner	78.6							
				61+	92.88		Masters	119.77		Other	140.2							
							PhD	188.67										
(Q13) *Waqf* is given for purposes that may be used by non-Muslim as well?							Elementary school	133.25										
				Up to 30	133.06		Primary school	138.75		Employed	123.97							
	Male	120.4		31to 40	107.4		Secondary school	126.21		Honorary	134.28		Yes	120.28		Yes	109.14	
	Female	120.58	0.983	41to 50	134.39	.020*	College	119.01	0.431	Unemployed	109.81	0.494	No	114.96	0.591	No	126.18	0.059
				51to 60	162		Specialist	94.5		Pensioner	85.3							
				61+	118		Masters	102.46		Other	123.71							
							PhD	101.33										
(Q14) It is necessary to execute waqif's will if such exist?							Elementary school	132.25										
				Up to 30	139.11		Primary school	108.13		Employed	116.59							
	Male	121.06		31to 40	112.74		Secondary school	109.88		Honorary	120.94		Yes	121.52		Yes	123.17	
	Female	120.03	0.903	41to 50	115.35	.022*	College	121.59	0.526	Unemployed	123.86	0.353	No	111.05	0.287	No	118.43	0.598
				51to 60	94.71		Specialist	113.6		Pensioner	170.2							
				61+	178.88		Masters	100.37		Other	132.41							
							PhD	109.33										

Question	Gender	Mean rank	Asymp. sig	Age	Mean rank	Asymp.sig	Education	Mean rank	Asymp. sig	Employment	Mean rank	Asymp.sig	Member of IC	Mean rank	Asym p.sig	Waqif	Mean rank	Asymp.sig
							Elementary school	111.19										
				Up to 30	114.39		Primary school	177		Employed	124.02							
	Male	129.35		31to 40	121.43		Secondary school	106.46		Honorary	139.56		Yes	121.96		Yes	128.98	
Q (15) *Waqf* can be sold seized or abused?	Female	114.96	0.078	41to 50	136.63	0.508	College	125.75	0.368	Unemployed	112.48	0.559	No	113.74	0.559	No	116.96	0.161
				51to 60	117.93		Specialist	119.4		Pensioner	148							
				61+	116.75		Masters	129.61		Other	114.93							
							PhD	128.67										
							Elementary school	134.55										
				Up to 30	139.09		Primary school	125.5		Employed	119.08							
	Male	111.52		31to 40	113.05		Secondary school	111.58		Honorary	118.67		Yes	114.47		Yes	102.45	
(Q16) *Waqf* cannot be returned to waqif?	Female	127.11	0.072	41to 50	118.07	.047*	College	113.99	0.514	Unemployed	133.3	0.343	No	131.46	0.343	No	127.97	.005*
				51to 60	122		Specialist	147.2		Pensioner	69.6							
				61+	62		Masters	115.1		Other	118.88							
							PhD	119.5										
							Elementary school	128.52										
				Up to 30	131.19		Primary school	111.63		Employed	120.35							
	Male	113.78		31to 40	118.77		Secondary school	142.27		Honorary	134.28		Yes	115.95		Yes	104.91	
(Q17) *Waqf* is an important institution for the promotion of the welfare of the society?	Female	127.06	0.07	41to 50	117.73	0.483	College	119.47	0.494	Unemployed	126.76	0.889	No	130.76	0.889	No	128.44	.002*
				51to 60	99.14		Specialist	105.8		Pensioner	113.6							
				61+	121.38		Masters	112.7		Other	117.18							
							PhD	82.5										
							Elementary school	99.81										
				Up to 30	110.67		Primary school	141.88		Employed	125.46							
	Male	126.89		31to 40	126.17		Secondary school	94.92		Honorary	151.89		Yes	120.07		Yes	125.88	
(Q19) *Waqf* does not bring benefits in the hereafter, *waqf* exclusively grants benefits on this world ?	Female	116.14	0.169	41to 50	133.27	0.092	College	128.62	.003*	Unemployed	117.3	0.095	No	117.66	0.095	No	117.76	0.322
				51to 60	96.71		Specialist	106.1		Pensioner	114.2							
				61+	74.63		Masters	147.15		Other	96.22							
							PhD	168										

Question	Gender	Mean rank	Asymp. sig	Age	Mean rank	Asymp.sig	Education	Mean rank	Asymp. sig	Employment	Mean rank	Asymp.sig	Memebr of IC	Mean rank	Asym p.sig	Waqif	Mean rank	Asymp.sig
							Elemntary shool	103.29					Yes	118.74		Yes	116.29	
				Up to 30	126.77		Primary school	99.38		Employed	118.16		No	119.85		No	121.86	
	Male	107.99		31to 40	119.47		Secondary school	142.63		Honorary	140.28							
(Q21) The waqf institution has given enough space and time for discussion in masjids?	Female	130.91	.006*	41to 50	107.06	0.173	College	127.16	0.084	Unemployed	120.8	0.498			0.91			0.528
				51to 60	164.43		Specialist	154.2		Pensioner	164.5							
				61+	147.75		Masters	115.8		Other	123.35							
							PhD	174										
					47.72		Elemntary shool	51										
				Up to 30	46.59		Primary school	40		Employed	48.86							
	Male	46.39		31to 40	50.07		Secondary school	40		Honorary	40		Yes	46.52		Yes	43.71	
(Q26) I'm happy to have endowed	Female	48.39	0.589	41to 50	64.13	0.389	College	49.08	0.634	Unemployed	47.05	0.877	No	48.38	0.659	No	49.45	0.175
				51to 60	40		Specialist	40		Pensioner	40							
				61+			Masters	40		Other	48.77							
							PhD	40										
					45.73		Elemntary shool	46.84										
				Up to 30	45.82		Primary school	14.5		Employed	45.97							
	Male	44.94		31to 40	47		Secondary school	33.13		Honorary	43.17		Yes	45.08		Yes	38.7	
(Q 27) The WDM anagement was kind and professional to me	Female	45.05	0.983	41to 50	50.38	0.503	College	46.91	0.474	Unemployed	42.56	0.969	No		0.704	No	47.7	0.14
				51to 60	14.5		Specialist	33.5		Pensioner	43.25							
				61+			Masters	52.75		Other	49.25							
							PhD	14.5										
					43.43		Elemntary shool	42.67										
				Up to 30	42.89		Primary school	17		Employed	41.68							
	Male	37.01		31to 40	40.23		Secondary school	17		Honorary	48.5		Yes	41.2		Yes	28.95	
(Q 28) All the conditions of my endowment are respected	Female	46.21	0.065	41to 50	53.13	0.474	College	45.05	0.338	Unemployed	41.03	0.938	No	42.38	0.834	No	46.37	.005*
				51to 60	17		Specialist	45.25		Pensioner	45.25							
				61+			Masters	42.17		Other	47.5							
							PhD	17										

Question	Gender	Mean rank	Asymp. sig	Age	Mean rank	Asymp.sig	Education	Mean rank	Asymp. sig	Employment	Mean rank	Asymp.sig	Memebr of IC	Mean rank	Asym p.sig	Waqif	Mean rank	Asymp.sig
(Q 29) The Islamic Community in B&H appreciates my contribution							Elementary school	46.44										
				Up to 30	45.71		Primary school	8		Employed	45.54							
	Male	43.59		31to 40	45.71		Secondary school	31.63		Honorary	50.17		Yes	45.4		Yes	42.96	
	Female	46.21	0.633	41to 50	46.2	0.847	College	46.16	0.353	Unemployed	43.16	0.981	No	41.96	0.561	No	46.37	0.571
				51to 60	47.4		Specialist	29.5		Pensioner	45							
				61+	37.25		Masters	50.14		Other	48.45							
					29.5		PhD	81										
(Q 32) Waqf institution has a great potential to become a respectful tool for the realization of the social justice and equality	Male						Elementary school	125.51										
	Female			Up to 30	119.52		Primary school	72.5		Employed	103.53							
		98.44		31to 40	96.49		Secondary school	105.59		Honorary	95.5		Yes	100.74		Yes	89.82	
		110.45	0.129	41to 50	104.21	0.124	College	96.79	0.113	Unemployed	100.5	0.468	No	110.6	..292	No	112.75	.005*
				51to 60	133.42		Specialist	98		Pensioner	99.4							
				61+	114.88		Masters	105.2		Other	126.2							
							PhD	107.5										
(Q 33) Waqf can play an important role in the economic development of B&H, as it can cover those sectors not sufficiently covered, or not covered at all by the state							Elementary school	124.36										
				Up to 30	112.56		Primary school	98.88		Employed	104.29							
				31to 40	100.46		Secondary school	124.73		Honorary	93.5							
	Male	103.5		41to 50	114.63		College	99.79		Unemployed	112.33		Yes	101.99		Yes	91.56	
	Female	109.51	0.431	51to 60	121.63	0.548	Specialist	104.8	0.173	Pensioner	129.2	0.717	No	115.1	0.158	No	114.82	.004*
				61+	115.25		Masters	93.91		Other	114.05							
							PhD	113.83										

Question	Gender	Mean rank	Asymp. sig	Age	Mean rank	Asymp.sig	Education	Mean rank	Asymp. sig	Employment	Mean rank	Asymp.sig	Memebr of IC	Mean rank	Asym p.sig	Waqif	Mean rank	Asymp.sig
(Q 34) The Islamic Community of B&H transparently reports its members and potential waqfis on the and distribution and expenses of waqf funds							Elementary school	98.83										
				Up to 30	111.59		Primary school	100.13		Employed	106.22							
	Male	103.5		31to 40	99.64		Secondary school	127.27		Honorary	82.71							
	Female	109.46	0.794	41to 50	109.05	0.682	College	100.28	0.114	Unemployed	95.35	0.394	Yes	103.07	0.972	Yes	105.8	0.706
				51to 60	109.83		Specialist	93.5		Pensioner	118.8		No	102.76		No	102.89	
				61+	118.5		Masters	129.77		Other	119.13							
							PhD	150.67										
(Q 35) Islamic Community in Bosnia and Herzegovina has a clear vision and strategy on the development of waqfs in B&H							Elementary school	89.02										
				Up to 30	110.73		Primary school	103.75		Employed	108.47							
	Male	110.35		31to 40	103.56		Secondary school	113.68		Honorary	111.71		Yes	104.21		Yes	104.15	
	Female	101.77	0.252	41to 50	109.29	0.478	College	107.28	.005*	Unemployed	96.13	0.771	No	105.59	0.88	No	106.32	0.778
				51to 60	82.25		Specialist	79.1		Pensioner	117.2							
				61+	141.13		Masters	145.18		Other	107.77							
							PhD	131.17										

References

Al Abadi, Abdusselam. 2001. "Consolidation and Development of Contemporary Waqf Institution." *Journal of Islamic Fiqh Academy* 1 (13): 536.

Al Sarkhasi, Shamsuddin. 1978. *Al Mabsut*. Bejrut: Daru al m'arifa.

Batuta, Ibn. 2001. *Travel in Asia and Africa (1325–1354)*. Translated by H. A. R Gibbon. London.

Belahija, Abduselam. 1933. *Uloga vakufa u verskom i svetovnom prosvećivanju naših muslimana*. Beograd: Štamparija Drag. Gregorića.

Boudjellal, M. 2005. "The Need for a New Approach of the Socio-Economic Developing Role of Waqf in the 21th Centry." In *Studies in Islamic Economics in 21st Century: Sharia Foundations, Theory and Institutions*, edited by M. Anwar and M. A. Haneef. Kuala Lumpur: Kulliyah of Economics and Management Sciences, International Islamic University of Malaysia.

Cajee, Z. 2008. *The Revival of Waqf in Muslim Communities: Implementation of the Recommendations of the International Waqf Conference South Africa, Cape Town, 2007*. Cape Town: Imam Sadiq University.

Cem, Behar. 2003. *A Neighborhood in Ottoman Istanbul*. New York: State University of New York.

Chapra, Umer M. 1992. *Islam and Economic Challenge*. Markfield: Islamic Foundation.

Ciampi, F., and N. Gordini. 2008. "Using Economic Financial Ratios for Small Enterprise Default Prediction Modelling: An Empirical Analysis." *Oxford Business & Economics Conference Program*, 1–21.

Cizakca, Munzir. 2000. *History of Philanthropic Foundation: Islamic World from the Seventh Century to the Present*. Istanbul: Bagazici University Press.

Cizakca, Murat. 1998. "Waqfs in History and Its Implications for Modern Islamic Economies." *Islamic Economic Studies* 6 (1).

Donia, Robert J. 1981. *Islam Under the Double EagleČ the Muslims of Bosnia and Herzegovina, 1878–1914*. Bouldewich. New York: East European Monographs.

Durmisevic, Enes. 2011. "Vakufi u Različitim Političkim Sistemima." U *Naučni Skup Vakufi u Bosni i Hercegovini Zbornik radova*. Sarajevo: Islamska Zajednica u Bosni i Hercegovini, Vakufska Direkcija.

Goksu, A., and A. Becic. 2012. "Awareness of Islamic Banking in Bosnia and Herzegovina." *International Journal of Finance and Economics* 100: 26–39.

Hadžić, Fikret. 2014. *Korištenje Islamskog bankarstva u BiH zavisi od raznih faktora*. Sarajevo: Novo Vrijeme.

Hadžić, Fikret, and Efendić, Velid. 2012. "Development of Interest-Free Banking in Bosnia and Herzegovina—Historical Aspects." Paper Presented at Business in Between Cultures—The Development of Islamic Finance, Sarajevo.

Hoexter, Miriam. 2002. "The Waqf and the Public Sphere." In *The Public Sphere in Muslim Societies*, edited by H. Miriam, S. N. Eisenstadt, and N. Levtzion. New York: New York University Press.

Islamic Financial Services Board (IFSB). 2005. "Guiding Principles of Risk Management." https://ifsb.org/standard/ifsb1.pdf. Accessed 28 October 2018.

Kahf, M. 1998. "Financing the Development of Awaqaf Property." Paper Presented at the Seminar on Development of Awaqf Organazied by Islamic Research and Training Institute (IRTI), Kuala Lumpur, Malaysia.

Kahf, M. 2003. *The Role of Waqf in Improving the Ummah Welfare*. Presented to the International Seminar Waqf as a Private Legal Body, Organized by Islamic University of North Sumatra, Medan, Indonesia, 6–7 January 2003. http://monzer.kahf.com/papers/english/ROLE_OF_WAQF_IN_THE_WELFARE_OF_THE_UMMAH.pdf.

Karcic, Fikret. 1983. "Međunarodno Regulisanje Vakufskih Pitanja u Jugoslovenskim Zemljama." *Anali Gazi Husrev-Begove Biblioteke* IX–X.

Karcic, Fikret. 2009. "Šerijatsko pravo-reformizam i izazovi modernosti." U *Hrestomatija Tskstova i Eseja*. Sarajevo: Bosnamuslimmedia.

Khan, M. Fahim. 1997. *Social Dimensions of Islamic Banks in Theory and Practice*. Jeddah: Islamic Research and Training Institute, Islamic Development Bank.

Krkic, Safet. 1989. *Uloga vakua u razvoju gradova u BiH*. Sarajevo: Biblioteka posebnih izdanja.

Malcom, Noel. 1994. *Bosnai: A Short History*. London: Papermac.

Muderis, Halilovic Nezim. 2013. "Historijat, Trenutno Stanje i Perspektive Vakufa." In *Vakufi u Bosni i Hercegovini, zbornik radova*, 20. Sarajevo: Islamska Zajednica u Bosni i Hercegovini, Vakufska Direkcija.

Omerdic, Muharem. 1999. *Prilozi izučavanja genocida nad Bošnjacima*. Sarajevo: El-Kalem.

Pirates, H., and H. Abdolmaleki. 2007. *Developing Awqaf Properties and Islamic Financial Engineering: A Conceptual and Empirical Analysis*. Singapur International Waqf Conference, Singapur International.

Zaimovic, S. 2013. "Petnaest Godina rada Vakufske Direkcije." In *Vakufi u Bosni i Hercegovini*. Sarajevo: Islamska Zajednica u Bosni i Hercegovini, Vakufska Direkcija.

Yalawae, T., and I.M. Tahir. 2003. *The Role of Islamic Institution in Acheiving Equility and Human Delevopment: Waqf or Endowment*. Kuala Lumpur: University Darul Iman (UDM).

CHAPTER 5

Efficient Diversification with Shariah-Compliant Stocks: Evidence from the South-East European Capital Markets

Azra Zaimović, Almira Arnaut-Berilo and Azra Osmanbegović

Key Topics

- Diversification
- Mean-variance analysis
- Shariah-compliant stock
- South-East Europe
- Islamic finance

A. Zaimović (✉) · A. Arnaut-Berilo
School of Economics and Business, University of Sarajevo, Sarajevo, Bosnia and Herzegovina
e-mail: azra.zaimovic@efsa.unsa.ba

A. Osmanbegović
ASA Banka, Sarajevo, Bosnia and Herzegovina

V. Efendic (ed.), *Islamic Finance Practices*,
https://doi.org/10.1007/978-3-030-34420-7_5

1 Introduction

In this paper, we aim to analyze the mean-variance efficiency of the mostly traded stocks from the seven South-East European (SEE) capital markets, included in the SEE link regional infrastructure platform. We screen stocks for Shariah-compliance in order to answer the question of how costly in terms of risk-return performance Shariah-compliance is. In addition, we explore the diversification potential of the regional (non-Shariah-compliant and Shariah-compliant) stocks and compare their efficiency with the efficiency of the stock market indices from the SEE and some European leading indices. From methodological point of view, we use AAOIFI stock screening criteria and Markowitz portfolio optimization method.

The paper is divided into five parts. Section 2, Literature Review, presents an overview of the results of previously conducted researches about efficient diversification and Shariah-compliant stock performances. In Sect. 3, we bring the methodology used for the analysis. Section 4 presents the data, their descriptive statistics, give the results of Shariah stock screening and identifies the diversification possibilities using Markowitz portfolio optimization method. Finally, brief summary and concluding remarks are given in Sect. 5.

2 Literature Review

Markowitz (1952) introduced the modern understanding of diversification and set the foundations for modern portfolio theory. He introduces efficient frontier or a set of efficient mean-variance portfolio combinations as those that have the highest return for the given level of risk and lowest risk for the given level of return (Markowitz and Todd 2000). Return is defined as a mean return of investment and risk as a square root of variance of returns. As the number of securities in portfolio increases, crucial impact on the variance of portfolio returns has covariance parts or variance–covariance matrix, meaning that efficient diversification relies heavily on low correlations. The total risk consists of the idiosyncratic risk and the systematic risk where idiosyncratic is the risk that can be diversified while systematic cannot be diversified. Therefore, diversification would represent combination of assets that reduces the idiosyncratic risk and leaves the group (portfolio of assets) only with, in ideal case, systematic risk (Bodie et al. 2009).

Zaimović et al. (2017) investigated portfolio diversification possibilities in the South-East European equity markets in the period from January 2006 till April 2016. They found that seven SEE equity markets offer substantial diversification opportunities among each other. On the other hand, their research showed limited diversification benefit from spreading out the investments form the SEE market to the leading world capital markets and vice versa, due to high integration of the SEE market with leading world markets.

In his study, Hussein (2004) examines whether the ethical investment has inferior performance compared with their unscreened counterparts through the comparison of the FTSE Global Islamic Index and counterpart index (FTSE All-World index). Research covers period (July 1996–August 2003). A comparison of the raw and risk-adjusted performance shows that the Islamic index performs as well as the FTSE All-World index over the entire period which means that the ethical screening does not have significant impact on the FTSE Global Islamic Index performance.

Jawadi et al. (2014) explore the financial performance of Islamic versus conventional indexes for three major regions: Europe, the USA and the World during the observed period 2000–2011 (including the period of the last global financial crisis). Authors calculated different performance ratios that vary according to type of risk (total, systematic and specific) and other restrictions (normal distribution, time-varying risk). Analysis shows interesting results—Islamic investments appear to outperform conventional, especially during the crisis period.

Ho et al. (2014) in their research also analyze risk-adjusted performance of global Islamic versus conventional share; the selected Islamic indices are matched with conventional indices. They investigated 12 major global Islamic and conventional indices from eight countries: the USA, the UK, Malaysia, Indonesia, Hong Kong, Switzerland, India and France. The data set period is from 2000 to 2011. Further, authors apply risk-adjusted measures of Sharpe ratio, Treynor Index and Jensen's Alpha in order to examine the performances between Islamic and conventional indices. The main findings in this study reveal that for the entire period, the majority of Islamic indices performed relatively better than their respective conventional indices.

Charles et al. (2015) investigate impact of the Shariah filtering criteria on the risk of Dow Jones Islamic indexes relative to their conventional counterparts (sample period 1996–2013). Results show that most of the Islamic indexes have higher level of risk than the conventional indexes.

They also find, according to different risk-adjusted performance measures, that the Islamic indexes either outperform the non-Islamic indexes or there is no notable difference in their performance. These findings can be explained as a result of less diversification in Islamic indexes, which means higher concentration risk in some sectors.

Banani and Hidayatun (2017) were exploring the performance of Islamic indices in two developing countries—Indonesia and Turkey, represented by Jakarta Islamic Index and Dow Jones Islamic Market Turkey, compared to their counterparts (sampling period of 2010 until 2014). The result based on three risk-adjusted performance ratios—Sharpe ratio, Treynor ratio and Jensen's Alpha—shows that Islamic index in Indonesia has insignificantly outperformed its counterpart LQ45 Index, while in Turkey Islamic index has insignificantly underperformed it counterpart Dow Jones Turkey Titans 20 index. According to these findings, Sharia-compliant did not remarkably affect the performance of Islamic index related to risk and return payoffs—both indices have resembling reward to risk and diversification benefits.

Ramadhan and Nugroho (2014), on the example of Indonesian capital market, examine the benefits of investing in Sharia capital market compared to the conventional one through the risk and return analysis using the modern portfolio theory approach. Research covers period from February 2013 until June 2014. The risk and return comparison of selected Indonesia's stock indices—Jakarta Islamic Index (Sharia capital market), Jakarta Composite Index (market) and LQ45 Index—shows that Jakarta Islamic Index's Sharpe ratio outperforms the Sharpe ratio of both—LQ45 Index and Jakarta Composite Index. Additionally, authors construct optimal portfolios by using portfolio optimization approach, to further elaborate the advantages of investing in Sharia capital market. The optimal portfolio constructed of selected Jakarta Islamic Index stocks outperforms the Jakarta Composite Index, LQ45 Index, and the Jakarta Islamic Index, in the comparison of Sharpe ratio.

Rifqi (2016) also investigated returns and risk performance of Jakarta Islamic Index (JII) in comparison with his counterpart—Jakarta Composite Index (JCI) using mean returns, standard deviation, Sharpe ratio, Treynor ratio, Jensen's Alpha and Value-at-Risk, and evaluate their results. Data sets cover period from January 2004 to May 2015. Results show that JII has lower raw and risk-adjusted returns in all sub-periods (except during pre-crisis), as shown by the mean returns, HPR, Sharpe and Treynor ratios, and Jensen's Alpha. Thus, there is a considerable cost associated with investing in Sharia way, in this case by using JII as investment benchmark instead of JCI.

Albaity and Ahmad (2008) provided research on the risk and return performance of the Kuala Lumpur Shariah Index (KLSI) and the Kuala Lumpur Composite Index (KLCI) during the period April 1999 to December 2005. They examined the performance of indexes using risk-adjusted return measures, and results, however, show that there is no evidence of significant statistical differences in risk-adjusted returns between Islamic and conventional stock market indices.

Jahromi (2013) analyzed risk, return and mean-variance efficiency of Islamic and non-Islamic stocks through the constructing of Islamic and non-Islamic indexes from the Malaysia stock market, using the screening methodology based on the Islamic business activity and financial ratio to separate Islamic and non-Islamic stock portfolios. Research includes data sets from January 1986 to March 2012. Research shows that Islamic stocks are more mean-variance efficient than non-Islamic stocks because they reduce risk for the same level of returns. Islamic stocks provide similar returns at a lower risk than non-Islamic stocks, as the standard deviation of Islamic stocks is lower than the standard deviation of non-Islamic stocks. Second, the Islamic portfolio is closer to the mean-variance efficient frontier and the minimum variance portfolio relative to the non-Islamic portfolio because it reduces risk for a similar level of expected returns.

Elias et al. (2015) on the example of Malaysian Shariah equities show that by applying Markowitz model, investor can achieve higher return at fixed level of tolerable risk as compared to benchmark index. They selected 50 Shariah-compliant stocks listed in FBM EMAS KLCI index (data sets from January 2009 until June 2011) for analysis. The performance of Sharia-compliant portfolio constructed by applying Markowitz model outperforms the FBM EMAS KLCI index. Their study is useful to investors in selecting portfolio of Shariah-compliant equities which are optimal and cost-effective.

Reddy and Fu (2014) examine whether there are differences in performance between the Shariah-compliant stocks and the conventional stocks listed on the Australian Stock Exchange (ASX) during the sampling period 2001–2013. Their findings show that there is a significant difference in performance of the Islamic and conventional stocks listed on the ASX in terms of risk—Islamic stocks are more risky; otherwise, the performance of the Islamic stocks tends to be close to the conventional stocks. The investigation of portfolios of two types of stocks using risk-adjusted ratios shows that the Islamic portfolio had higher adjusted returns (Sharpe ratio) than the conventional stocks.

3 Methodology

The classical Markowitz portfolio model is used to determine the efficient return-risk combination, i.e., efficient frontier (EF).[1] Efficient frontier is convex curve and lies between the portfolio with minimal standard deviation and the portfolio with maximum rate of return (mean).

Model includes portfolio expected return

$$\overline{R}_p = \sum_{i=1}^{n} \overline{R}_i x_i \tag{1}$$

and portfolio variances

$$\sigma_p^2 = \sum_{j=1}^{n}\sum_{i=1}^{n} x_j x_i \mathrm{Cov}(R_i, R_j) \tag{2}$$

where investments satisfy the investment constraints:

$$\sum_{i=1}^{n} x_i = 1 \tag{3}$$

and no negativity conditions $x_i \geq 0, \quad i = \overline{1, n}$.

If the investor considers investing in a portfolio, with a pre-determined value of expected return on investment E, we have additional constraint:

$$\sum_{i=1}^{n} \bar{R}_i x_i = E. \tag{4}$$

As a result, model presents the investment vectors that provide the absolutely minimum portfolio return variance $\sigma^2_{\min}$ with the pre-set return E. By choosing randomly expected return of investment in the range $\bar{R}_{\min} \leq E \leq \bar{R}_{\max}$,[2] we can determine the efficient set of the observed security (Arnaut-Berilo and Zaimović 2012).

Square root of portfolio variance is used as measure of portfolio risk, and it includes correlations between equity return. Markowitz argued that low or negative correlations will eliminate portfolio risk, measured by σ_p^2.

Shariah screening refers to the process of identifying Shariah-compliant investments. Standard Shariah mandate is broadly based on the AAOIFI Shariah standards defined for screening equities. Companies are only to be considered compliant from a sector perspective if the total sum of non-permissible income derived from Shariah-impermissible activities is less than 5% of their total income. Impermissible products and services are alcohol, pork-related products, conventional financial services like banks and insurance companies, gold and silver hedging, entertainment (e.g., hotel, casinos, gambling, etc.), tobacco and weapons and defense.

Second level of Shariah screening based on financial ratios is intended to remove companies based on debt and interest income levels in their balance sheets. The financial ratios used to screen the companies are as follows:

1. Interest-bearing cash and short-term investments/12-month daily avg. market capitalization <30%
2. Interest-bearing debt/12-month daily avg. market capitalization <30%
3. Liquid assets including cash, short-term investments and receivables/assets <70%.

Companies that operate according to the Shariah and/or have a Shariah board supervising their activities are to be considered automatically compliant such as Islamic banks and Islamic insurance companies.

4 Results and Discussion

We perform our analysis on a sample of selected stocks quoted on the seven SEE stock exchanges: Ljubljana Stock Exchange (LJSE), Zagreb Stock Exchange (ZSE), Sarajevo Stock Exchange (SASE), Banja Luka Stock Exchange (BLSE), Belgrade Stock Exchange (BELEX), Bulgarian Stock Exchange (BSE-Sofia) and Macedonian Stock Exchange (MSE). Firstly, stock selection criteria are set as follows:

1. The stocks must be constituent of the reprehensive stock index.

2. Liquidity must satisfy the requirement that the stocks are traded at least 75% of possible trading days during the observed five years period (November 2012–October 2017).
3. A minimum of one and a maximum of three stocks can be represented from one stock exchange.

According to aforementioned criteria, 17 stocks of seven capital markets were selected, with three stocks of each stock exchange with exception of the Banja Luka and Sarajevo stock exchanges where only one stock meets the liquidity criteria. The selected sample is shown in Table 1.

In the selected sample, three stocks are from the telecom and pharmaceutical industry, two stocks are from the banking and oil distribution industry and one from the other industries. Stocks from Croatia have very high liquidity, and more of them meet the established liquidity requirement. So, three stocks (components of the CROBEX 10) with the largest market capitalization were chosen, with the note that Valamar Riviera (RIVP) was replaced with Podravka (PODR). RIVP is not included in the sample because of discontinued trading from August to November 2013. Also, in a sample of Bulgarian stock market, investment fund—Advance Terrafund (6A6) was replaced with the CB Central Cooperative Bank (4CF).

The second phase of stock selection (Shariah-compliant screening) was made according to AAOIFI standards, which includes industry and financial criteria. Below are presented the basic characteristics of the business of the selected companies.

Alkaloid AD Skopje (ALK) is leading Macedonian pharmaceutical company which operates through four segments: pharmaceuticals, chemicals, cosmetics and botanicals. It offers medicines for human, pharmaceutical raw materials and veterinary drugs, as well as over the counter drugs, dietary supplements, medical devices and others.

Komercijalna banka (KMB) is one of the leading banks in Macedonia. Komercijalna banka provides various banking products and services for individuals and legal entities in Macedonia and internationally.

Makpetrol AD Skopje (MPT) is a Macedonian company, specialized in the wholesale and retail of petroleum products. Makpetrol distributes and trades oils, biofuels and oil products in Macedonia and internationally.

Aerodrom Nikola Tesla a.d. Beograd (AERO) is a leading airport operator in Serbia. It provides airport services in the Belgrade Nikola Tesla Airport, such as ground handling of aircraft, passengers, goods and mail in

Table 1 Selected sample

No.	*Company*	*Ticker*	*Industry*	*Stock exchange*
1.	Alkaloid AD, Skopje	ALK	Pharmaceuticals	MSE
2.	Komercijalna banka AD, Skopje	KMB	Banking	MSE
3.	Makpetrol AD, Skopje	MPT	Retail (oil distribution)	MSE
4.	Aerodrom Nikola Tesla a.d., Beograd	AERO	Air transport	BELEX
5.	Energoprojekt holding a.d., Beograd	ENHL	Construction services	BELEX
6.	NIS a.d., Novi Sad	NIIS	Oil & gas operations	BELEX
7.	Hrvatski Telekom d.d., Zagreb	HT	Telecommunications	ZSE
8.	Adris grupa d.d., Rovinj	ADRS2	Diversified holdings	ZSE
9.	Podravka prehrambena industrija d.d., Koprivnica	PODR	Food processing	ZSE
10.	Krka d.d., Novo mesto	KRKG	Pharmaceuticals	LJSE
11.	Petrol d.d., Ljubljana	PETG	Retail (oil distribution)	LJSE
12.	Zavarovalnica Triglav d.d., Ljubljana	ZVTG	Insurance	LJSE
13.	BH Telecom d.d., Sarajevo	BHTSR	Telecommunications	SASE
14.	Telekom Srpske a.d., Banja Luka	TLKM-R-A	Telecommunications	BLSE
15.	CB Central Cooperative Bank AD-Sofia	4CF	Banking	BSE
16.	Chimimport AD-Sofia	6C4	Finance & insurance	BSE
17.	Sopharma AD-Sofia	3JR	Pharmaceuticals	BSE

Source Authors

domestic and international traffic, maintenance of runway maneuvering areas, equipment and installations enabling aviation activities and cargo warehouse management.

Energoprojekt Holding a.d. Beograd (ENHL) engages in design, engineering and construction activities in Serbia and internationally. The company operates through: planning and research, construction and fitting and other segments. It offers research, consulting, engineering, strategic planning, design and project management services in the fields of hydroenergy, drinking water supply, purification of wastewater, melioration systems, and infrastructural facilities and systems, telecommunications and environmental protection.

Naftna Industrija Srbije a.d. Beograd (NIIS) is an integrated oil company which engages in the exploration, development and production of crude oil and gas in Serbia. It is also involved in the production of refined petroleum products, petroleum products and gas trading, and electricity generation and trading.

Hrvatski Telekom d.d. Zagreb (HT) provides various telecommunication services to residential and corporate customers, small- and medium-sized businesses and public sector customers in Croatia and abroad. The company offers mobile telecommunication services, fixed telephony services, including fixed telephone line access and network services, and also provides Internet services.

Adris grupa d.d. Rovinj (ADRS2) engages in the tourism, insurance, trade and agriculture activities in Croatia and abroad. It operates through insurance, tourism and other segments.

Podravka d.d. Koprivnica (PODR) is a Croatia-based company primarily engaged in the food processing industry. A well-diversified product portfolio divided into two main business areas: food (primary) and pharmaceuticals.

Krka d.d. Novo Mesto (KRKG) is a Slovenian pharmaceutical company. The company operates through four segments: prescription pharmaceuticals, non-prescription products, animal health products and health resort and tourist services.

Petrol d.d. Ljubljana (PETG) is a Slovenian company engaged in the provision of oil and other energy products. The company operates through two lead segments: oil and merchandise sales and energy activities. The oil and merchandise sales segment consists of sale of oil and petroleum products and sale of supplementary merchandise. The energy activities segment consists of sale and distribution of gas, generation, sale and distribution of electricity and heat, etc.

Zavarovalnica Triglav d.d. Ljubljana (ZVTG) is the leading insurance—financial group in Slovenia and in the Adria region and one of the leading groups in South-East Europe. The key business lines are asset management and insurance.

BH Telecom d.d. Sarajevo (BHTSR) is the biggest telecom operator in Bosna and Herzegovina. Company provides telecommunications services to consumers and business clients including fixed telephony, mobile telephony, Internet access and IPTV integrated services.

Telekom Srpske a.d. Banja Luka (TLKM-R-A) is one of the three dominant telecom operators on the Bosnia and Herzegovina territory, which offers telecommunication services in the field of mobile telephony, fixed telephony, Internet and data.

Central Cooperative Bank AD-Sofia (4CF) is a Bulgarian commercial bank that provides retail banking, corporate banking and other financial services. The bank is operational through the network of branches and offices located across Bulgaria, as well as one office in Cyprus.

Chimimport AD-Sofia (6C4) is a Bulgarian holding company. It is engaged in the acquisition of stocks, the restructuring and management of its subsidiaries, as well as in capital investments and financing of other enterprises, where the company has direct stockholdings.

Sopharma AD-Sofia (3JR) is the biggest vertically integrated human health pharmaceutical group in Bulgaria. The group's operations include: production of pharmaceutical products, mostly generics, production of medical supplies and consumables, distribution of medical products, drugs, herbal substances, food supplements, vitamins, equipment and cosmetics.

In accordance with the industry compliance criteria, 11 of 17 companies passed the industry screening, i.e., ZVTG, KMB, ADRS2, PODR, 4CF and 6C4 are excluded from the further analysis.

We performed qualitative industry screening of the sample companies based on their business operations. The core business of sample companies was free from *riba*, *gharar* and *maysir*, activities which are not permissible from Shariah perspective (Bin Mahfouz and Ahmed 2014).

We excluded conventional banks and conventional insurance companies, and companies which core business was producing or selling Shariah-impermissible products or services, such as tobacco, alcohol, weaponry and casino games. We didn't perform detailed analysis whether or not all their products or services are Shariah-compliant. More detailed analysis of companies operations is needed if real investment decision in Shariah-compliant stocks (SCSs) would be made. The result of further and final selection based on the financial criteria is the final set (SEE-8) of eight stocks (Table 2): ALK, AERO, ENHL, HT, KRKG, BHTSR, TLKM-R-A and 3JR.

In order to explore the diversification potential of the South-East European stock market and compare its efficiency with the efficiency of the regional stock market indices and some European leading indices, we performed mean-variance analysis. Formed efficient portfolios consisting of all sample stocks (SEE-17) and Shariah-compliant stocks (SEE-8) are presented in Fig. 1. Curved lines represent efficient frontiers created from 17 SEE stocks (SEE-17) and eight Shariah-compliant stocks (SEE-8). Efficient portfolio risk varies from 1.89 to 6.77% (SEE-8), i.e., from

Table 2 Shariah-compliant screening—financial criteria

		Criteria 1		*Criteria 2*		*Criteria 3*	
		Interest-bearing cash and short-term investments/12-month average daily market capitalization <30%		*Interest-bearing debt/12-month average daily market capitalization <30%*		*Liquid assets including cash, short-term investments and receivables/assets <70%*	
No.	*Ticker*	*2017 (%)*	*2012 (%)*	*2017 (%)*	*2012 (%)*	*2017 (%)*	*2012 (%)*
1.	ALK	0.84	1.08	5.11	9.57	22.42	24.51
2.	AERO	11.50	12.55	2.53	11.09	19.80	14.28
3.	ENHL	3.24	26.73	10.25	9.61	16.83	12.62
4.	HT	21.17	20.54	0.02	0.00	31.94	36.46
5.	KRKG	3.80	4.76	1.51	4.38	29.43	32.71
6.	BHTSR	28.62	12.67	0.04	0.46	27.93	21.54
7.	TLKM-R-A	6.31	15.53	9.80	5.59	14.68	20.75
8.	3JR	1.19	0.76	15.57	62.63	18.40	34.96
9.	MPT	13.11	9.94	95.45	105.90	14.47	22.65
10.	NIIS	29.11	9.95	63.01	39.29	17.59	20.68
11.	PETG	3.43	7.43	59.71	132.17	7.72	23.43
12.	ZVTG	–	–	–	–	–	–
13.	KMB	–	–	–	–	–	–
14.	ADRS2	–	–	–	–	–	–
15.	PODR	–	–	–	–	–	–
16.	4CF	–	–	–	–	–	–
17.	6C4	–	–	–	–	–	–

Source Authors

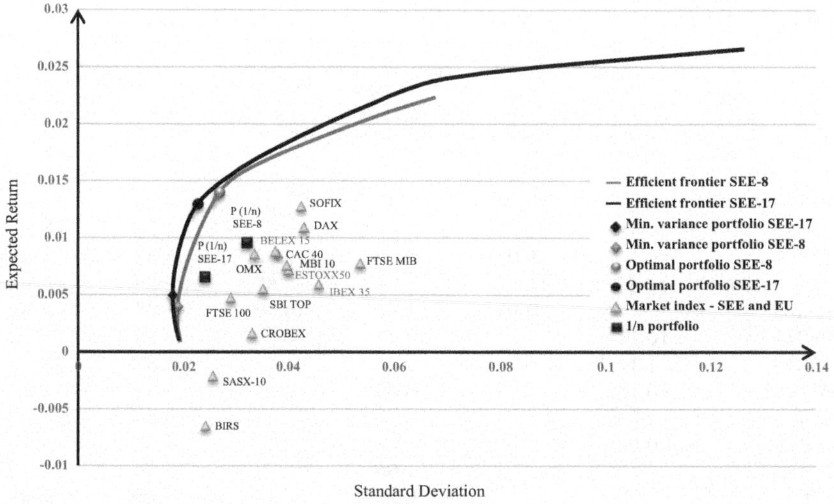

Fig. 1 Efficient frontiers SEE-8, SEE-17, 1/n and index portfolios (*Source* Authors)

1.80 to 12.65% (SEE-17), while the returns vary from 0.3 to 2.23% (SEE-8), i.e., from 0.5 to 2.66% (SEE-17).

For the further analysis of mean-variance efficiency of SEE-8 and SEE-17, we consider minimum variance portfolios ($P3_{min.v}$ and $P5_{min.v}$), maximum Sharpe ratio portfolios[3] ($P13_{opt}$ and $P14_{opt}$) and portfolios created on the simple diversification criteria, i.e., equally weighted portfolios ($P_{1/n}$ SEE-8 and $P_{1/n}$ SEE-17). The structure of these portfolios is presented in Table 3.

In Table 4, we present mean-variance performance and Sharpe ratio of portfolios of our interest and also risk-return profile of seven SEE (BIRS, SASX-10, SBI TOP, MBI 10, CROBEX, BELEX 15, SOFIX) and seven European stock market indices (CAC 40, DAX, FTSE 100, FTSE MIB, IBEX 35, OMX NORDIC 40, EUROSTOXX 50).

Based on the Sharpe ratio and the graphical interpretation on Fig. 1, we can see that selected efficient portfolios P13, P14, P5 and P3 dominate in mean-variance sense over the regional and selected European stock market indices.

Table 3 Structure of characteristic SEE-17 and SEE-8 portfolios

Ticker	*Optimal portfolio*		*Min. variance portfolio*		*1/n portfolio*	
	P13 (SEE-17) (%)	*P14 (SEE-8) (%)*	*P5 (SEE-17) (%)*	*P3 (SEE-8) (%)*	*P1/n (SEE-17) (%)*	*P1/n (SEE-8) (%)*
ALK	40.03	53.24	28.33	27.63	5.88	12.50
AERO	14.48	21.83			5.88	12.50
ENHL	4.74	8.08	3.20	3.26	5.88	12.50
3JR	11.43	16.82	7.86	7.87	5.88	12.50
KRKG		0.04	11.30	14.69	5.88	12.50
PETG	16.11		12.11		5.88	
ZVTG	1.12				5.88	
ADRS2	10.18		0.82		5.88	
4CF	1.83				5.88	
MPT	0.07				5.88	
KMB			1.06		5.88	
HT			0.43	7.18	5.88	12.50
PODR			4.88		5.88	
BHTSR			17.42	23.29	5.88	12.50
6C4					5.88	
TLKM-R-A			12.59	16.07	5.88	12.50
NIIS					5.88	
Total	100.00	100.00	100.00	100.00	100.00	100.00
No. of stocks	9	5	11	7	17	8

Source Authors

This leads us to the conclusion that stocks from SEE region offer significant diversification opportunities to the European investors. By spreading their stock market investments to SEE region, European investors could obtain better risk-return profiles. However, it should be noted that mean-variance analysis is based on historical performance of stocks, i.e., if the ex-post data are good in assessment of future returns regional stock portfolios might perform even better than the leading European indices. Zaimović and Arnaut-Berilo (2015) in their research about diversification possibilities between equity markets in Bosnia and Herzegovina and Germany found that even though German market is more mean-variance efficient than the Bosnian, spreading investments among these markets can decrease portfolio risk.

Table 4 Characteristic SEE-17 and SEE-8 portfolios, index portfolios

Portfolio	*Standard deviation (%)*	*Expected return (%)*	*Sharpe ratio (%)*
$P13_{opt}$ (SEE-17)	2.28	1.30	56.97
$P14_{opt}$ (SEE-8)	2.70	1.40	51.95
$P5_{min.v}$ (SEE-17)	1.80	0.50	27.77
$P3_{min.v}$ (SEE-8)	1.89	0.30	15.88
$P_{1/n}$ (SEE-17)	3.24	0.96	29.61
$P_{1/n}$ (SEE-8)	2.42	0.66	27.21
SASX-10	2.58	−0.21	−8.16
BIRS	2.43	−0.65	−26.66
SBI TOP	3.54	0.55	15.63
MBI 10	3.99	0.76	19.07
CROBEX	3.33	0.16	4.94
BELEX 15	3.77	0.88	23.41
SOFIX	4.27	1.28	29.99
CAC 40	3.83	0.86	22.54
DAX	4.31	1.10	25.42
FTSE 100	2.92	0.47	16.25
FTSE MIB	5.37	0.78	14.58
IBEX 35	4.59	0.59	12.95
OMX NORDIC 40	3.38	0.86	25.50
EURO STOXX 50	4.03	0.72	17.90

Source Authors

Efficient frontiers of SEE-8 and SEE-17 stocks overlap in some parts or are very close to each other (Fig. 1). In order to test the hypothesis do SCSs investors sacrifice any return for the given level of risk, we generate random portfolios from all sample stocks and investigate their performance. We test how many randomly selected portfolios formed from the total sets of 17 selected SEE stocks were contained within the convex set formed by the efficient frontier of eight SCSs, Fig. 2.

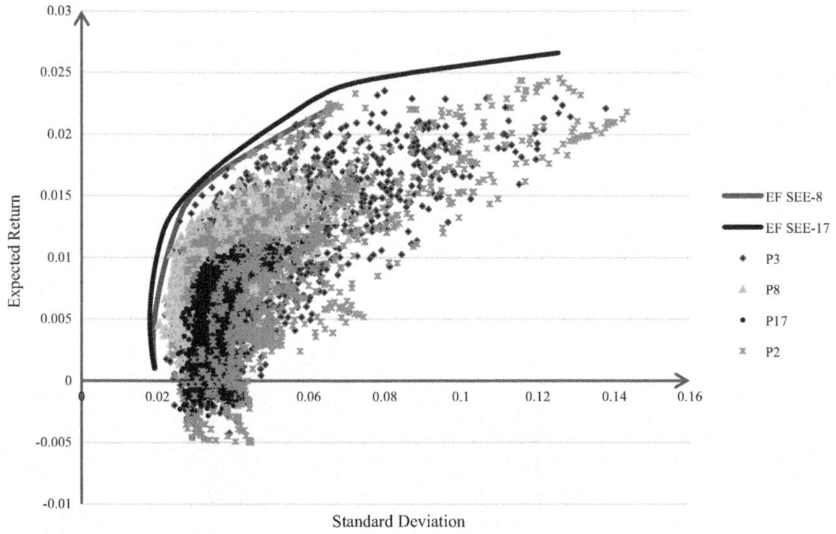

Fig. 2 Efficient frontiers SEE-8, SEE-17, 1/n and other portfolios (*Source* Authors)

The longer curve in Fig. 2 represents efficient frontier derived from SEE-17 selected assets, and the shorter one represents efficient frontier derived from eight SCSs (SEE-8). We created 10,000 portfolios made up of any 2, 3, 8 and 17 stocks, with random weights. Asterisk markers in the graph represent 1000 randomly selected portfolios formed from two randomly selected stocks. Circle markers represent 3000 randomly selected portfolios formed from 17 randomly selected stocks. Triangle markers represent 3000 randomly selected portfolios formed from eight randomly selected stocks, and diamond markers represent 3000 randomly selected portfolios formed from three randomly selected stocks.

Our results (Fig. 2) show that only five portfolios out of 10,000 generated portfolios could be found outside the convex region bounded by the efficient line of Shariah-compliant stocks (SEE-8). These five portfolios are in upper part of the efficient frontier showing that non-Shariah-compliant stocks have impact on the extreme returns but not on the risk reduction. Based on these results, we can conclude that efficient portfolios composed of eight SCSs dominate over 99.95% of all portfolios composed of any 2, 3, 8 and 17 stocks in terms of Markowitz definition of dominancy.

In addition, we checked domination of efficient set over the randomly selected portfolio consisting of more than four stocks (five, six, etc.), and we concluded that these mean-variance portfolios are far more homogeneous, so the percentage of SCSs dominancy could only be higher. These results are not present in the paper, but there are available on request.

We emphasize that SCSs enable investors to achieve the same minimum risk portfolios like all sample stocks. This leads us to the conclusion that sufficient diversification can be achieved by investments in SCSs. Returns higher than those that could be created with SCSs are accompanied by a huge increase in risk. On the other hand, extreme returns, which are connected to large risk exposure, cannot be obtained with SCSs.

5 Conclusion

We analyzed the mean-variance performance of 17 mostly traded stocks from the seven SEE capital markets in five years period, from November 2012 until October 2017, in order to investigate diversification possibilities of the regional stock exchanges. Our empirical findings show that SEE region offers significant diversification opportunities to the European investors. By spreading their stock market investments to SEE region, European investors could obtain better risk-return profiles. If ex-post data are good in assessment of expected returns, regional stock portfolios might outperform leading European indices. However, it should be noted that Markowitz mean-variance analysis is based on historical data and also that this research covers 17 mostly traded stocks, i.e., regional blue-chip stocks. This might help in understanding these findings.

With the aim to contribute to the empirical findings of the performance of Shariah-compliant stocks (SCSs), we performed the Shariah-compliant stock screening based on the AAIOFI methodology and find eight stocks out of 17 being SCSs. We created 10,000 portfolios made up of any 2, 3, 8 and 17 stocks, with random weights. Efficient portfolios composed of eight SCSs dominate over 99.95% of all possible portfolios composed of sample stocks. We conclude that investors in SCSs do not sacrifice any return for the given level of risk in comparison with investors in all sample stocks, i.e., SCS investors can obtain the same risk-return efficiency as other investors.

The main constraint of our research is that we analyzed 17 stocks from seven SEE stock markets, which does not give us the possibility to generalize our findings. We based our methodological approach on the fact that randomly selected 15–20 stocks diversify most systematic risk in national stock markets, i.e., variance of the portfolio is being reduced to the systematic risk level and there is no additional risk-reducing benefit of expending further portfolios. Due to nonsynchronous trading problems, we did not randomly select stocks. Instead, we took the most liquid stocks; these stocks can be seen as blue-chip stocks of these markets. It is possible that larger sample could result in even better performing efficient portfolios, moving the efficient frontier more north-west in the coordinate system. In that case, our findings about diversification opportunities would be even strengthen.

We recommend expending sample in further investigation of the performance of regional Shariah-compliant and non-Shariah-compliant stocks.

Notes

1. The mean-variance combination of a portfolio is efficient if there are no other combinations with the same return, and a lower variance, or the same variance and higher return.
2. If the following is true $E > \bar{R}_{\max}$, the model would be unsolvable, and if $E < \bar{R}_{\min}$, then the solution to the system (1–4) would not be an element of the efficient set, where $\bar{R}_{\min}$ and $\bar{R}_{\max}$ correspond to the efficient portfolio with the lowest variance and maximum return, respectively.
3. Adjusted Sharpe ratio calculated with the assumption that risk-free rate is zero.

References

Albaity, M., and Ahmad, R. 2008. Performance of Syariah and composite indices: Evidence from Bursa Malaysia. *Asian Academy of Management Journal of Accounting and Finance* 4 (1): 23–43.

Arnaut-Berilo, A., and Zaimović, A. 2012. How efficient are Bosnian stock market indices? *Eastern European Economics Journal* 50 (1): 26–45.

Banani, A., and Hidayatun, N. A. 2017. Performance of Islamic indices: Risk adjusted returns of Sharia compliant stocks on Jakarta Islamic Index and Dow Jones Islamic Turkey. *Journal Economics & Business Atmajaya Indonesia* 1 (1): 1–18.

Bin Mahfouz, S., and Ahmed, H. 2014. Sharia investment screening criteria: A critical review. *Journal of King Abdulaziz University: Islamic Economics* 27 (1): 3–38.

Bodie, Z., Alex K., and Marcus A. J. 2009. *Essentials of Investments*, 8th Edition. McGraw-Hill: New York, NY.

Charles, A., Darné, O., and Pop, A. 2015. Risk and ethical investment: Empirical evidence from Dow Jones Islamic Indexes. *Research in International Business and Finance* 35: 33–56.

Elias, S. M., Razak, M. Z., and Kamil, K. H. 2015. Investment strategies in Malaysian Shariah-compliant equities with transaction costs. *Ulum Islamiyyah Journal* 13: 179–196.

Ho, C. S. F., Rahman, N. A. A., Yusuf, N. H. M., and Zamzamin, Z. 2014. Performance of global Islamic versus conventional share indices: International evidence. *Pacific-Basin Finance Journal* 28: 110–121.

Hussein, K. 2004. Ethical investment: Empirical evidence from FTSE Islamic Index. *Islamic Economic Studies* 12 (1): 21–40.

Jahromi, M. 2013. Risk, return, and mean-variance-efficiency of Islamic and non-Islamic stocks. Paper presented at the 26th Australasian Finance and Banking Conference of the UNSW Business School, Sydney, Australia, December.

Jawadi, F., Jawadi, N., and Louhichi, W. 2014. Conventional and Islamic stock price performance: An empirical investigation. *International Economics* 137: 73–87.

Markowitz, H. 1952. Portfolio selection. *The Journal of Finance* 7 (1): 77–91.

Markowitz, H., and Todd, P. 2000. *Mean-Variance Analysis in Portfolio Choice and Capital Markets*. Frank J. Fabozzi Associates: New Hope, PA.

Ramadhan, M. R., and Nugroho, A. B. 2014. Advantages of Investing in Sharia Financial Instruments Using Modern Portfolio Theory Approach. Paper presented at the 7th Asia Pacific Business Research (APBR) Conference of the World Business Institute (WBI) Australia, Singapore, August.

Reddy, K., and Fu, M. 2014. Does Shariah compliant stocks perform better than the conventional stocks? A comparative study stocks listed on the Australian stock exchange. *Asian Journal of Finance & Accounting* 6 (2): 155–170.

Rifqi, M. 2016. The cost of Sharia investing: Comparative empirical study in Indonesian stock market. *Journal of Emerging Economies & Islamic Research* 4 (1): 1–13.

Zaimović, A., and Arnaut-Berilo, A. 2015. Risk diversification between stock markets in Germany and Bosnia and Herzegovina. *South East European Journal of Economics and Business* 9 (1): 30–36.

Zaimović, A., Arnaut-Berilo, A., and Mustafić, A. 2017. Portfolio diversification in the South-East European equity markets. *South East European Journal of Economics and Business* 12 (1): 126–135.

CHAPTER 6

Credit Risk Assessment for an Islamic Bank in Bosnia and Herzegovina

Migdat Hodžić and Nerma Saračević

1 Introduction

Credit risk management is the subject of many worldwide researches, for both conventional and Islamic financial institutions. Credit risk research is valuable for banking management, investors, business partners, and state regulatory agencies, but also globally, especially after major financial crises that negatively impacted the economic growth of developed and developing countries. After the growth of the Islamic banking market and the Great Depression of 2008, the Islamic banking sector has increased its interest in the analysis of credit risk, which resulted in scientific studies analyzing the factors affecting the creditworthiness of clients. Taking into account the specificity of Islamic financing, as well as compliance with the Sharia Law, the number of scientific studies on this topic is relatively

M. Hodžić
International University of Sarajevo, Sarajevo, Bosnia and Herzegovina
e-mail: mhodzic@ius.edu.ba

N. Saračević (✉)
University of J.J. Strossmayer, Osijek, Croatia
e-mail: nermasa@bih.net.ba

V. Efendic (ed.), *Islamic Finance Practices*,
https://doi.org/10.1007/978-3-030-34420-7_6

small. Different regulatory rules in countries with developed Islamic banking have limited research to individual countries, and these are mainly the result of analysis of individual Islamic banking markets, mainly related to the probability of default (PD) or non-performing loans (NPL) of Islamic banks, but not their clients.

The reason for a very small number of studies is the difficulties in accessing financial and other data from Islamic bank clients. The lack of access to data is particularly present for small- and medium-sized enterprises which are not required to publicly publish their financial results and other business-related information.

With the credit risk assessment methods in Islamic banks being insufficiently researched, in the literature we can frequently find studies analyzing the models for the most accurate corporate predictions of failure in conventional banks using different modeling techniques. Statistical methods are most frequently used.

Classical statistical methods are discriminant analysis, regression analysis, neural network, and decision trees. Below is an overview of the most common models or methods, the authors of some of the researches and the countries where the models or methods on selected databases were used (Table 1).

Islamic Financial Service Board (IFSB) defines credit risk as "the potential that a counterparty fails to meet its obligations in accordance with agreed terms. This definition is applicable to Institutions Offering Islamic Financial Services (IIFS) managing the financing exposures of receivables and leases (e.g., *Murābahah, Diminishing Mushārakah, and Ijārah*) and working capital financing transactions/projects (e.g., *Salam*, *Istisnā'*, or *Muḍārabah*)" (2005, p. 6).

One of the first works (Abdou et al. 2014) on tools for predicting the creditworthiness in Islamic finance was made on the basis of 487 applications of natural persons in an Islamic Finance House in the UK. Three methods were used to create a scoring model of discriminant analysis (DA), logistic regression (LR), and multi-layer perceptron (MP) neural network.

The results showed that the LR model has the highest rate of correct classification applications, while MP has an advantage over other techniques in the prediction of rejected requests for loans, as well as the lowest cost incorrect classification. The MP model identifies monthly costs, age, and marital status as key elements that are significant in the decision-making process.

Table 1 The overview of some of the authors, statistical methods, models, and countries

Model	*Country*	*Authors*
Z score model	USA	Altman (1968)
	Greece	Gerantonis and Christopoulos (2009)
	Kenya	Odipo and Sitati (2010)
	Ghana	Appiah (2011)
	Turkey	Ali (2007)
	International	Altman (1984)
ZETA model		Altman et al. (1977)
Logit and probit model	Taiwan	Shen and Huang (2010)
	Korea	Nam and Jinn (2000)
Logistic regression	Croatia	Šarlija et al. (2009)
	Spain	Andreev (2005)
	Bosnia and Herzegovina	Memić (2015)
Discriminant analysis	Italy	Ciampi and Gordini (2008)
	Czech Republic	Dvoracek et al. (2008)
Decision trees	USA	Galindo and Tamayo (2000)
Neural network	Croatia	Zekic-Susac et al. (2004)
	USA (Credit Union)	Desai et al. (1997)

Source Authors' work

In their work on analyzing financial ratios in discriminating between healthy and distressed companies (Saracevic and Sarlija 2017), compared to previous researches, profitability ratios and activity ratios are the most important indicators in distinguishing healthy and distressed companies. The methods used are the statistical methods of Mann–Whitney test for years 2009 and 2010 and a *t*-test for years 2011–2013. Mann–Whitney method was used because of a relatively small number of clients and *t*-test from 2011 due to changes in accounting standards for the creation of balance sheet positions of clients. In order to obtain comparable results, different methodologies were used. This analysis is a step forward in the development of a scoring model based on SME clients of an Islamic bank financed by diminishing Musharakah.

Fuzzy logic methods for credit scoring model compliant with Sharia were used by Sidik et al. (2013). Their score is obtained by using an IT2FS algorithm based on two variables (sum of late day) and (installment amount) for each customer. They proposed two scenarios and concluded that they are fairer than the conventional method. Based on their proposed business model, "*the fines will be imposed if and only if the customer cannot prove that the delay was due to inadvertence*" (Sidik et al. 2013).

2 Basel Rules Review and Summary

Basel II represents the concept of calculating the capital adequacy of a bank, thereby defining the rules in the measurement and management of the risks the bank is exposed during its business. As the capital represents protection from unexpected losses and it is the basis of the bank growth, Basel II rules define how much the value of a bank's own capital is sufficient to cover unexpected losses.

Since the primary function of own capital is to protect the bank from the risk of insolvency, the banks are obliged to adjust this value to the risk assets of the bank. Capital adequacy is the basis for growth, development, and stability of the bank. If the bank's own capital is too low, there is a danger of the inability to absorb losses, the likelihood of bankruptcy increases, but the client deposits are also jeopardized. In the event that capital is too high, it is impossible to achieve a sufficiently high rate of return on sources of funds, thus leading to a business profitability problem (Šarlija and Gereč 2008).

As can be seen from Table 2, Basel II (Basel Committee on Banking Supervision 2003) is based on three pillars:

Table 2 3 Pillars of Basel II

Pillar 1	*Pillar 2*	*Pillar 3*
Minimum capital requirements: – Risk management incentives – New operational risk capital charge – Risk-weighted assets (RWA) for credit more risk-sensitive – Market risk largely uncharged	**Supervisory review**: – Solvency reports – Regulatory review – Capital determination – Regulatory intervention – Addresses risks that are not captured in Pillar 1 like concentration and liquidity risks	**Market discipline**: – Minimum disclosure requirements – Scope – Capital transparency – Capital adequacy – Risk measurement and management – Risk profiling

Source Bakiciol et al. (2013)

- Minimum capital requirement (Pillar 1),
- Supervisory review (Pillar 2),
- Market discipline (Pillar 3).

The minimum capital requirements consist of basic capital increased by retained earnings, after-tax reserves, and additional capital. The calculation of the capital adequacy ratio is made by dividing the regulatory capital by the amount of the total exposure to risk.

Unlike the previous rules, the operational risk is added to the credit and market risks. For banks operating in Bosnia and Herzegovina, the minimum capital adequacy ratio is 16%.

Even though the other risks are covered by these standards (2003), the credit risk, being the most important, is measured by the methods set in accordance with Basel II:

1. Standardized approach (SA),
2. Foundation internal rating-based (IRB) approach,
3. Advanced internal rating-based (IRB) approach.

The SA is similar to the Basel I standard based on the formation of fixed risk weights that are arranged in accordance with the type of a claim. Supervisors are responsible for determining the weights, and the banks are bound to adopt and implement them. Risk-weighted claims are categorized by the SA into claims from government institutions, banks, companies, households, and claims secured by mortgages on real estate. It is allowed to determine the risk weight in accordance with the rating determined by an external credit rating agency, verified by the national regulator. In addition to this, the Basel II standards define more weights for companies, and risky household claims are secured in the form of mortgages on residential property of a certain risk-weight level from 35 to 75%. Treatment of small and medium enterprises can be included in the framework of the retail segment and may be subject to various other criteria (Basel Committee on Banking Supervision 2003).

Internal rating-based (IRB) approach differs from the SA in terms of the responsibility for customer risk assessment. Namely, the sole responsibility for customer risk assessment, according to the IRB approach, lies with the bank, while the SA approach puts the exclusive responsibility at the regulator (Basel Committee on Banking Supervision 2003).

The bank classifies the claims in 5 risk groups:

1. Companies,
2. State institutions,
3. Banks,
4. Retail,
5. Equity securities.

For each group of the claims, the bank sets: elements of risk, the calculation of risk-weighted assets that are transformed in capital requirements, and minimum requirements relating to the adoption of standards that banks must have in order to apply the IRB approach.

According to Basel II standards, the basic risk elements are:

1. Probability of default—the probability that the borrower will not pay contractual obligations,
2. Loss given default (LGD)—the percentage loss rate exposure if the company happens default event,
3. Exposure at default (EAD)—the outstanding debt at the time of default,
4. Maturity—"the maximum remaining time (in years) that the obligor is permitted to take to fully discharge its contractual obligation, including principal, interest, and fees, under the terms of loan agreement" (Train 2018).

Foundation IRB approach and advanced IRB approach differ in responsibility for determination of risk elements, i.e., whether the bank or the regulator sets the basic elements as shown in Table 3.

Table 3 The difference between FIRB and AIRB

	PD	*LGD*	*EAD*	*M*
Foundation IRB	Bank	Regulator	Regulator	Regulator
Advanced IRB	Bank	Bank	Bank	Bank

Source Consultative Document; Overview of the New Basel Capital Accord (2003)

Basel III emerged as a response to the global economic crisis; also as a purpose of the Basel Committee to strengthen the banking regulatory framework with a group of reform measures which would make the banking sector resistant to the stresses caused by the financial and economic shocks. This regulatory framework implies improving risk management in banks and increasing their transparency in work. The first version of Basel III framework was issued in December 2010, revised version in June 2011, and the latest version, "Final post-crisis reforms," in December 2017. From the period of the first version of Basel III until the current version, several documents were adopted, completing the regulatory framework in order to protect banks against unexpected losses.

The basic elements of Basel III are:

- Increase of minimum capital requirements,
- Better management of bank liquidity,
- Banking protection against the likelihood of bank deposit withdrawal by a large number of clients (Bank Run).

Consequently, Basel III defines the regulatory capital, consisted of,

- Common Equity Tier 1—common shares, retained earnings, and other reserves,
- Additional Tier 1—capital instruments with no fixed maturity,
- Tier 2—subordinated debt and general loan-loss reserves.

The capital ratio is calculated as the amount of regulatory capital divided by the amount of risk assets. The higher the amount of risk assets, the greater the capital is needed and vice versa.

$$\text{Risk-based capital ratios} = \frac{\text{Regulatory capital}}{\text{Risk-weighted assets}}$$

In terms of capital requirements, Table 4 presents the difference between the Basel II and Basel III.

Table 4 Capital adequacy assessment—Basel II and Basel III

	Basel II (%)	*Base III (%)*
Common equity (risk-weighted assets after deduction)	2	4.5
Total common equity	4	7
Countercyclical buffer	–	0–2.5

Source Basel Committee on Banking Supervision (2017)

In order to strengthen the profitability position and control of debt of the banks, Basel III introduces a minimum leverage ratio which is calculated by dividing the Tier 1 capital to average total consolidated assets of the bank. Banks should maintain a leverage ratio up 3%.

$$\text{Leverage ratio} = \frac{\text{Tier1}}{\begin{array}{c}\text{On- and off-balance sheet exposures} \\ \text{(including derivates, repos, and other secururities} \\ \text{financing transaction)}\end{array}} \geq 3\%$$

“A leverage ratio constrains the build-up of debt to fund banks’ investment and activities (bank leverage), reducing the risk of a deleveraging spiral during downturns” (Basel Committee on Banking Supervision 2017).

Regarding to short-time liquidity position, liquidity risk management of the banks, among the other things, imposes the obligation of the banks to provide minimum coverage ratio of liquidity (Liquidity Coverage Ratio—LCR), which represents the ratio between the levels of the protective layer of liquidity and total net liquidity outflows during the period of stress for a period of 30 calendar days.

In terms of view, the long-term liquidity position Basel III introduces the net stable ratio of funding establishes a management standard of structural or long-term liquidity. It requires that the available amount of stable funding exceeds the required amount of stable funding in a period of 1 year of crisis.

Available stable sources (capital, long-term loans, stable deposits) must be larger than the required stable sources that are assessed on the basis of the maturity and quality of the approved loans.

3 Banking Legislation in Bosnia and Herzegovina

Banks in B&H, due to more rigorous requirements from Regulator, have more favorable indicators of capitalization. Indicators which measure the ratio of the amount of capital and assets are significantly higher than in Western European countries. In B&H this ratio is about 16%, while in Western European countries it is commonly found to be around 11% or 12%. It is a consequence of more stringent capital requirements, which were introduced precisely in order to provide additional resistance to the banking system in the "younger" markets.

The share of B&H banks within foreign banking groups is very small and ranges between 3 and 5%. Banks in B&H are dealing with traditional banking, and their assets did not include potentially dangerous assets, but almost exclusively loans for domestic economy. Therefore, their assets are not jeopardized by a significant decrease in the value of shares or real estate in countries with overpriced real estate prices.

Due to the very harsh demands regarding maturity compliance for B&H banks, fortunately, they did not have the flexibility to borrow for a short time and to provide long-term loans. Banks are heavily funded on the basis of domestic deposits, and this is a model that has survived in the USA where investment banks bought such banks (Centralna Banka Bosne i Hercegovine 2018).

Given the legislation applied in the banking sector, the only Islamic bank has found its place in this market and it is developing with very stable steps.

In terms of strengthening stability and resistance of B&H banks to possible capital risks, liquidity risks, market risks, and other significant risks related to the specificities of each bank's operation individually at the beginning of 2019, the Banking Agency of B&H adopted a decision on the Internal Capital Adequacy Assessment Process and Internal Liquidity Adequacy Assessment Process which will be implemented from January 2020 (Agencija za Bankarstvo Federacije Bosne i Hercegovine 2019).

4 Islamic Banking Data

The data used in this paper are the basis of financial statements—the balance sheets of an Islamic bank's client in B&H. Based on the available data, the authors calculated financial ratios that indicate the difference between healthy companies and those that show signs of instability. In

Table 5 Overview of financial ratios

Liquidity ratios	
CR—Current ratio	QR—Quick ratio
CshR—Cash ratio	CA/TA—Current assets/total assets
FA/NCp—Fixed assets/net capital	FSR—Financial stability ratios long-term assets/capital+long-term liabilities
Leverage ratios	
Csh/CA—Cash/current assets	WC/TA—Working capital/total assets
ShtFD/TD—Short-term financial debt/total debt	ShtD/TD—Short-term debt/total debt
DR—Debt ratio	Gearing—Liabilities(debt)/equity
LofCI—Level of coverage I	LofCII—Level of coverage II
LofCIII—Level of coverage III	
Activity ratios	
TATR—Total assets turnover ratio	STATR—ST assets turnover ratio
LTATR—LT assets turnover ratio	TrofRcvb—Turnover ratio of receivables
CollDay—Collection period in days	DaySlsInv—Days' sales in inventory
OpCy—Operating cycle	TrofInv—Turnover ratio of investment
Efficiency ratios	
Inv/CoGS—Inventories/cost of goods sold	EofTAc—Efficiency of total activity
EofBAc—Efficiency of business activity (sales activity)	EofFinOp—Efficiency of financial operations
EofOpAc—Efficiency of operating activity	GrMg—Gross margin
Profitability ratios	
GrMg—Gross margin	OpMg—Operating margin
NproMg—Net profit margin	ROA—Return on assets
ROA1—Gross ROA	ROE—Return on equity
CoIncR—Cost income ratio	Prof ExSrc—Profitability of external sources of financing
RE/TA—Retained earnings/total assets	

Source Authors' work

the calculation, 419 companies' data were used ranging from 2009 to 2013. Each individual financial ratio was analyzed. The financial ratios are divided into five groups as shown in Table 5:

- Liquidity ratios,
- Leverage ratios,

- Activity ratios,
- Efficiency ratios,
- Profitability ratios.

4.1 Research Methodology and Model Building

During the research of which companies are distressed or healthy and formation of the model, the following statistical methods were used:

- the Mann–Whitney test for years 2009 and 2010,
- *t*-test for years 2011–2013,
- LR for building the model.

The Mann–Whitney test is a non-parametric test for the difference in distribution (Sheskin 2004); the *t*-test is a parametric test for testing the difference in means (ibid., p. 375). The Mann–Whitney statistical method was used because of the relatively small number of customers and *t*-test due to changes in accounting standards since 2011 year to create balance sheet positions for clients. In order to obtain comparable results, different methodologies were used.

Logistic regression is defined usually as statistical method which is an integral part of any data analysis that deals with the linkage between dependent and independent variables. Its aim is to find a model that is best adapted to the data, which contain only those independent variables that affect the outcome of the dependent variable and which describes the relationship between dependent and independent variables. U izradi ovog modela LR ima za cilj izračunati koje varijable mogu ukazati na moguće kašnjenje u otplati ugovornih obaveza klijenta. In developing this model, LR aims at determining which variables may indicate a possible delay in repayment of client's contractual obligations.

5 Credit Risk Assessment Model

The model should predict the PD of the clients of an Islamic bank, based on an available database, which was formed in the time period of five years. The classification of clients to distressed or healthy is based on the delay in repayment of contractual obligations, for a period of time longer than 90 days. Dependent variables are 0 and 1, where 0 indicates a healthy company and 1 a distressed company.

Available data for this study consisted of 419 clients of an Islamic bank in B&H. As indicated in Table 6, through the total number of companies, the financial statements (balance sheet, income statement) of the companies were available during the period from 2009 to 2013, but not for all companies over the entire period.

The LR model classification results using the 9 predictor variables and the area under curve (AUC) was used from the standpoint of measuring the accuracy of the model.

"The area under curve (AUC), referred to as index of accuracy (A) or concordance index, is a perfect performance metric for ROC curve. Higher the area under curve, better the prediction power of the model" (Analytics Vidhya Content Team 2015).

The best accuracy of the calculated model is in the case when the AUC is

$$0.5 < AUC < 1.0. \text{ In this model, } AUC = 0.71.$$

Kolmogorov–Smirnov (K–S) statistic is one of the most widely used measures for the predictive strength of credit risk models. The K–S statistic is usually calculated for LR results in order to obtain the model quality indication. "*K-S or Kolmogorov-Smirnov chart measures performance of classification models. More accurately, K-S is a measure of the degree of separation between the positive and negative distributions. The K-S is 100 if the scores partition the population into two separate groups in which one group contains all the positives and the other all the negatives. On the other hand, if the model cannot differentiate between positives and negatives, then it is as if the model selects cases randomly from the population. The K-S would be 0. In most classification models the K-S will fall between 0 and 100, and that the higher the value the better the model is at separating the positive from negative cases*" (Model Evaluation—Classification 2018).

In our case, K–S = −0.46 which shows good quality model's prediction.

Table 7 shows the percentage of accuracy of the tested model for the prediction of healthy and distressed companies on the basis dataset from an Islamic bank in B&H. The results showed 71.4% accuracy of the company health forecasting model in the analizyed periods, which is a good

Table 6 Descriptive analysis

Year	*2009*		*2010*		*2011*		*2012*		*2013*	
	%	*N*	%	*N*	%	*N*	%	*N*	*N*	%
Healthy	89.69	174	89.59	241	83.59	219	82.62	328	75.86	176
Distressed	10.31	20	16.41	28	16.41	43	17.38	69	24.14	56
Total	100	194	100	269	100	262	100	397	100	232

Source Saracevic and Sarlija (2017)

Table 7 The rate of accuracy of tested model

Total rate of hits	71.4%
Rate of hits for variable 0	83.3%
Rate of hits for variable 1	62.5%

Source Authors' work

Table 8 List of predictor variables and their importance used in building the scoring model

Variable	*Code*	*Ratio-type*	*Importance*
Financial stability ratios	FSR_1	Liquidity	0.253
Level of coverage I	LofCI_1	Leverage	0.644
Total assets turnover ratio	TATR_1	Activity	0.122
LT assets turnover ratio	LTATR_1	Activity	0.531
Turnover ratio of receivables	TRofRcvb_1	Activity	0.413
TrofInv—Turnover ratio of investment	TRofInv_1	Activity	0.314
Inventories/cost of goods sold	Inv_CoGS_1	Efficiency	0.221
Gross margin	GrMg_1	Profitability	0.039
Return on assets	ROA_1	Profitability	0.092

Source Authors' work

level of prediction. Table 8 summarizes 9 predictors and their importance for the accuracy of the model.

As Table 8 shows, the most important variables for the model are LofCI, LTATR, TRofRcvb TRofInv, FSR, Inv_CoGS, and TATR with contribution weightings of 0.644, 0.531, 0.431, 0.314, 0.253, and 0.221, respectively. On the other hand, the least influential variables are ROA and GrMg with contribution weightings of 0.092 and 0.039. The most influential variables are from the group of leverage and activity ratios, as well as a bit less importance carries the variables from the group of liquidity and efficiency ratios.

6 Future Work

One of the areas of future research related to Islamic banking credit risk prediction is incorporation, in a precise mathematical way, of so-called soft (subjective expert opinions) data. In practice, soft data are used in credit risk assessment in all banks, but in an ad hoc way, based on credit expert personal opinion or with soft coding as hard and then plugging into statistical methods. In our other work in progress (Brkić et al. 2018), we presented a soft–hard data fusion approach for default probability prediction improvement for general banking environment. This approach can be readily extended to Islamic banking area with the proper soft data modeling. The database was from a B&H commercial bank with 300+ commercial customer data used. In this context, we are looking to obtain a larger database of Islamic credit risk-related customers, so our approach can be validated further.

7 Conclusion

The aim of this research is to form a model that would serve as a tool for better credit risk management, based on existing clients of an Islamic bank from B&H. Prediction of PD based on financial indicators, and a 5-year time series, is based on statistical methods, and the final model is formed on the basis of LR results.

Comparing the previous works with the results obtained in this research, it became evident that financially troubled businesses have a lower level of liquidity ratios, higher leverage ratios, and lower ratio of activity compared to financially healthy companies. In the resulting credit risk assessment model, we have leverage and activity ratios with higher contribution weightings than other from groups of efficiency, liquidity, and profitability ratios. As in the previous study (Saracevic and Sarlija 2017), it has been shown that the ratio of activity is very important for the analysis of Islamic bank companies in our results, although it can be very effective for commercial banks as well.

References

Abdou, H., Alam, S., & Mulkeen, J. (2014). Would Credit Scoring Work for Islamic Finance? A Neural Network Approach. *International Journal of Islamic and Middle Eastern Finance and Management, 7*(1), 112–125.

Agencija za Bankarstvo Federacije Bosne i Hercegovine. (2019, February 27). https://www.fba.ba/images/banke_podzakonski_2/odluka_o_ilaap_i_icaap_nakon_uo_-_27_02_19_bos_-_za_web.pdf.

Ali, S. (2007). Financial Distress and Bank Failure: Lessons from Closure of Ihlas Finance in Turkey. *Islamic Economic Studies, 14*(1/2), 1–52.

Altman, E. (1968). Financial Ratios, Discriminant Analysis and the Prediction of Corporate Bankruptcy. *Journal of Finance, 23*, 589–609.

Altman, E. I. (1984). The Success of Business Failure Prediction Models: An International Survey. *Journal of Banking and Finance, 8*(2), 171–198.

Altman, E., Haldeman, R., & Narayanan, P. (1977). Zeta Analysis: A New Model to Identify Bankruptcy Risk of Corporations. *Journal of Banking & Finance, 1*, 29–54.

Analytics Vidhya Content Team. (2015, November 1). https://www.analyticsvidhya.com. Retrieved May 25, 2018, from https://www.analyticsvidhya.com.

Andreev, Y. A. (2005). *Predicting Financial Distress of Spanish Companies.* Barcelona: Department of Business Economics, University of Barcelona.

Appiah, K. (2011). Corporate Failure Prediction: Some Empirical Evidence from Listed Firms in Ghana. *China-USA Business Review, 10*(1), 32–41.

Bakiciol, T., Cojocaru-Durand, N., & Lu, D. (2013). *Basel II.* Retrieved November 29, 2018, from https://docplayer.net/8509081-Basel-ii-tamer-bakiciol-nicolas-cojocaru-durand-dongxu-lu.html.

Basel Committee on Banking Supervision. (2003). *Consultative Document; Overview of the New Basel Capital Accord.* Basel: Bank for International Settlements.

Basel Committee on Banking Supervision. (2017, December 7). *Basel III: International Regulatory Framework for Banks.* Retrieved June 25, 2018, from https://www.bis.org/bcbs/basel3.hTM.

Brkić, S., Hodzic, M., & Dzanic, E. (2018). *Soft-Hard Data Fusion via Uncertainty Balance Principle—Evidence from Corporate Credit Risk Assessment in Commercial Banking.* Work in Progress. Sarajevo.

Centralna Banka Bosne i Hercegovine. (2018). https://www.cbbh.ba/press/ShowNews/562?lang=hr. Retrieved from https://www.cbbh.ba/press/ShowNews/562?lang=hr.

Ciampi, F., & Gordini, N. (2008). Using Economic Financial Ratios for Small Enterprise Default Prediction Modelling: An Empirical Analysis. In *Oxford Business & Economics Conference Program* (pp. 1–21).

Desai, V. S., Crook, J. N., & Overstreet, G. A. (1997). Credit Scoring Models in Credit Union Environment Using Neural Network and Generic Algorithms. *IMA Journal of Mathematic Applied in Business & Industry, 8*, 323–346.

Dvoracek, I., Sousedikova, R., & Domaracka, L. (2008). Industrial Enterprises Bankruptcy Forecasting. *Metalurgija, 47*, 33–36.

Galindo, J., & Tamayo, P. (2000). Credit Risk Assessment Using Statistical and Machine Learning: Basic Methodology and Risk Modeling Applications. *Computational Economics, 15*, 107–143.

Gerantonis, N., & Christopoulos, A. (2009). Can Altman Z-score Models Predict Business Failures in Greece. *Research Journal of International Studies, 12*(21), 21–28.

Islamic Financial Services Board (IFSB). (2005). *Guiding Principles of Risk Management.* Retrieved October 28, 2018, from https://ifsb.org/standard/ifsb1.pdf.

Memić, D. (2015). Assessing Credit Default Using Logistic Regression and Multiple Discriminant Analysis: Empirical Evidence from Bosnia and Herzegovina. *Interdisciplinary Description of Complex Systems, 13*(1), *128–153.*

Model Evaluation—Classification. (2018, May 25). Retrieved from https://www.saedsayad.com/model_evaluation_c.htm.

Nam, J. H., & Jinn, T. (2000). Bankruptcy Prediction: Evidence from Korean Listed Companies During the IMF Crisis. *Journal of International Financial Management and Accounting, 11*(3), 178–197.

Odipo, M., & Sitati, A. (2010). *Evaluation of Applicability of Altman's Revised Model in Prediction of Financial Distress: A Case of Companies Quoted in the Nairobi Stock Exchange.* Retrieved October 28, 2018, from https://profiles.uonbi.ac.ke/olipo_martin/files/business_failure_prediction_18_sept_2010.pdf.

Ohlson, J. (1980). Financial Ratios and Probabilistic Prediction of Bankruptcy. *Journal of Accounting Research, 18*(1), 109–131.

Saracevic, N., & Sarlija, N. (2017). The Usefulness of Financial Ratios in Discriminating Between Healthy and Distressed Companies: A Case of an Islamic bank. In V. Efendic, F. Hadzic, & H. Izhar (Eds.), *Critical Issues and Challenges in Islamic Economics and Finance Development* (pp. 137–155). Berlin: Springer-Verlag Gmbh.

Šarlija, N., Šoric, K., & Vojvodic, V. (2009). *Logistic Regression and Multicriteria Decision Making in Credit Scoring.* Retrieved October 28, 2018, from http://bib.irb.hr/datoteka/466476.sarlija_soric_vlah_vojvodic.pdf.

Šarlija, N., & Gereč, A. Z. (2008). *Kratak pregled Basela 2.* Retrieved November 29, 2018, from http://www.efos.unios.hr/nsarlija/wp-content/uploads/sites/88/2013/04/kratak-pregled-basela-2.pdf.

Shen, H. C., & Huang, Y. B. (2010). The Prediction of Default with Outliers: Robust Logistic Regression. In *Handbook of Quantitative Finance and Risk Management* (pp. 965–977). Boston: Springer.

Sheskin, J. D. (2004). *Handbook of Parametric and Nonparametric Statistical Procedures.* Washington, DC: Chapman & Hall and CRC.

Sidik, G. K., Djatna, T., & Buono, A. (2013). An It2fs Model for Sharia Credit Scoring: Analysis & Design. *Journal of Information System, 8*(2), 58–66.

Train, F. (2018). *Effective Maturity in Basel II.* Retrieved January 10, 2019, from https://financetrain.com.

Zekic-Susac, M., Sarlija, N., & Bensic, M. (2004). Small Business Credit Scoring: A Comparison of Logistic Regression, Neural Network and Decision Tree Models. In *Proceedings of the 26th International Conference on Information Technology Interfaces* (pp. 265–270). Cavtat, Dubrovnik, Croatia.

Zmijewski, E. M. (1984). Methodological Issues Related to the Estimation of Financial Distress Prediction Models. *Journal of Accounting Research, 12*, 59–82.

CHAPTER 7

Market Rent Value as a Basis for Profit Margin Calculation in Home Financings Based on Diminishing Musharakah with Ijarah: Possibilities for Implementation in Bosnia and Herzegovina

Anisa Lojo-Bajrić and Fikret Hadžić

Key Topics

- Calculation of Profit Margin for Diminishing Musharakah Financings in Bosna Bank International Sarajevo
- Use of Market Rent for Profit Margin Calculation

Fikret Hadžić: Deceased.

A. Lojo-Bajrić (✉)
Bosna Bank International Sarajevo, Sarajevo, Bosnia and Herzegovina
e-mail: anisa.lojo@bbi.ba

V. Efendic (ed.), *Islamic Finance Practices*,
https://doi.org/10.1007/978-3-030-34420-7_7

- Possibilities of Implementation of Market Rent Based Profit Margin Model in Bosnia and Herzegovina

1 Introduction

Diminishing musharakah with ijarah represents one of the most frequently used models in Islamic finance. It is very popular due to flexibility it provides for both banks and clients and transparency in terms of profit and loss sharing. Islamic banks across the world use diminishing musharakah as a basis for different financial products, especially for home purchase financings.

Islamic banks calculate profit margin in a manner similar to conventional banks, using *different criteria, such as risk premium, costs of sources, client's rating, competition margins etc.* They also use LIBOR or EURIBOR as benchmarks for financings with variable profit margin. Profit margin could also be calculated using a market rent as a base, since the revenue a bank receives from a client is actually rent for its share in real estate bought through diminishing musharakah financing. In this paper we shall analyse possibilities to use market rent as a base for profit margin in Bosna Bank International Sarajevo (BBI), the first bank in South East Europe and the only in Bosnia and Herzegovina that operates according to Shariah.

Despite certain limitations in Bosnia and Herzegovina market, such as the double taxation for real estates problem, diminishing musharakah with ijarah is a frequently used model in Bosna Bank International Sarajevo, which was the first bank in Southeast Europe that operated in line with Islamic principles. We can even say it represents the backbone of the banks' assets, since most of its financings are based on this particular model. BBI uses the diminishing musharakah model for the following types of personal financings: financings for home purchase, building or renovation, mortgage financings, car financings, and cash financings through financial partnership in real estate. It is also used as a basis for

F. Hadžić
School of Economics and Business in Sarajevo,
University of Sarajevo, Sarajevo, Bosnia and Herzegovina

most of corporate financings, including fixed assets purchase financings, car, real estate, land, equipment financings, etc.

2 Profit Margin Calculation in Diminishing Musharakah and Ijarah Financings in Bosna Bank International

Profit margins for all types of financings in Bosna Bank International are defined by the following: costs of funds, risk premium, the banks 'profitability goals (specially ROA and ROE), terms on domestic and international capital markets, competitors' offers in BIH market, legal provisions (Bosna Bank International 2015, 2017c).

Profit margins for natural persons for all types of financings, including those based on diminishing musharakah, depend on: financing amount, repayment period, client's credit rating, previous collaboration with the client, collateral, and other criteria (Bosna Bank International 2015, 2017c, p. 5).

BBI uses proportional method for profit margin calculation for all financings based on diminishing musharakah and ijarah. Profit margin is variable, linked to six-month EURIBOR or LIBOR. That means that the profit margin, i.e., monthly rent a client pays for using the bank's share in real estate (or other asset) consists of two parts: fixed mark-up, defined by different factors, and six-month EURIBOR or LIBOR (Bosna Bank International 2015, 2017c).

Many Islamic banks use EURIBOR or LIBOR as reference indices for profit margin for their financings. Shariah experts in general approve of their use, despite the fact that they are actually interest rates. They explain that, despite this fact, both EURIBOR and LIBOR actually represent only frequently used and commonly accepted referent values that do affect the price, but not the model of financing, that is a base for relationship between a bank and a client.

However, even though they are acceptable as reference indices according to Shariah and local legislation, LIBOR and EURIBOR are not ideal basis for profit margin creation for BBI. This is because neither LIBOR nor EURIBOR reflect interest rates, rentals for real estates, prices of real estates or other economic variables on Bosnia and Herzegovina market, although they are indirectly linked to them and could affect their levels. These indices, hence, are not directly linked to any type of diminishing musharakah financing and do not influence its profitability. Furthermore, even though many relevant institutions regularly give projections of these rates, their value in the future is quite unpredictable, for both the client and the bank. There is also problem of reputational risk for Islamic banks because of the use interest rate, that is forbidden in Islam, as benchmark. Therefore, in order to find the most suitable model, it is necessary to also consider other bases for profit margin creation for diminishing musharakah and ijarah financing.

3 Market Rent as a Basis for Profit Margin Calculation

When we analyze the way home financings based on diminishing musharakah and ijarah operate, we can conclude that market rent for real estate properties is the most logical basis to use for profit margin calculation, since the rent itself is actually what bank and client get as a profit from partnership in real estate shared ownership.

Using the market value of the rent as the basis for calculating the bank‘s profit is also justified from the Islamic standpoint, and it is even preferable to the model used by conventional banks, which is based on trying to maximize the bank's profit. This model, as explained by Rama et al. (n.d.), contributes to general prosperity of the society, as the Shariah and Islamic economics propagate, because, in accordance with the value of the real estate, a higher rent is charged to clients who are prepared to pay more and buy luxury real estate which costs more, whereas it also enables less wealthy people to buy a house or apartment at a lower rent, in accordance with their abilities and location, size and age of the real estate they are buying, which is often cheaper and less attractive in the market. This contributes to a more just division of income and eventually has positive effects on economic prosperity.

Profit margin variability is also important question to analyze, since most of home financings based on diminishing musharakah with ijarah are long-term.

Tahir (2013) advises avoiding variable profit margin arrangement because, as he states, according to Shariah law, the rent should be fixed during the entire period of partnership. He suggests that, if Islamic banks expect future market trends will have negative implications for their business, they should include such predictions in their initially defined rent or make shorter-term partnership contracts, which significantly reduces the competitiveness of Islamic banks compared to conventional banks, and which can jeopardize its business operations in the long term.

Bendjilali and Khan (1995) and Muhamed Taqi Usmani, on the other hand, believe that, in order to avoid uncertainty (*gharar*), rent shared by the financer and the client can be linked to a certain index such as rent index and home price index (as cited by Meera and Abdul Razak 2009). Usmani (2003) states that rent must be defined for the whole rental period at the time of conclusion of the contract. He believes that, if the bank wants to agree on a variable rent with the client, it can only do so if, at the time of signing the lease contract, they agree in advance on rents for each period of the lease during which variable rent would be applied, whether the change agreed upon is expressed in precisely defined percentages (e.g., 3% growth each six months) or the new rent or new percentage of the profit margin is defined (e.g., after six months, new rent totals BAM 500 per month). In his opinion, it is not acceptable to agree when signing the contract that at a certain point the bank would determine the rent without consulting the client (Usmani 2003). From this, we can conclude that if the bank and the client at the time of signing the contract for partnership based on diminishing musharakah, agree that the rent will periodically, in precisely defined periods, be adjusted to certain official indicators, such as the rent index, such model of determining the rent is acceptable and a variable profit margin can be defined in this case.

4 Comparison of the Existing Method of Calculating the Profit Margin at BBI and the Model Based on Market Rent Value

Annuity amount in commercial banks depends on: amount of loan, repayment period and defined interest rate. Annuity amount P is calculated using the formula below, where P is the monthly payment, i is the monthly interest rate, PV is the present value of the loan, i.e., of the client's debt, and n is the repayment period:

$$P = \frac{i * PV}{1 - (1 + i)^{-n}} \text{ or } P = \frac{i(1 + i)^n PV}{(1 + i)^n - 1}$$

Calculating the monthly payments with diminishing musharakah, if the basis for the calculation is market rent and market value of real estate, can be done using the formula adapted to the formula used by conventional banks, where M is the total monthly payment, x is the rent rate, B_0 is the bank's share in partnership, which is analogous to principal in conventional banking, and n is the repayment period (Meera and Abdul Razak 2009):

$$M = \frac{x(1+x)^n B_0}{(1+x)^n - 1}$$

where rent rate x is calculated using this formula:

$$x = \text{total monthly rentprice of the real estate} \times 100$$

This formula is actually the same as the aforementioned formula used by conventional banks, and the formula currently used by BBI to calculate the client's monthly payment for financings based on diminishing musharakah:

$$M = \frac{p(1+p)^n B_0}{(1+p)^n - 1}$$

In the aforementioned formula, rent rate x is actually profit margin p on a monthly level, created based on factors described above. For easier differentiation, we will use p for this indicator and x for rent rate based on market rent.

The only difference between the three formulas mentioned above is the calculation of monthly rate, which is calculated based on monthly rent and price of the real estate in the second formula, whereas conventional banks and BBI use many more factors, such as source costs, risk factors for certain client categories, etc. to calculate their interest/profit rate. In the case of variable interest rate/profit margin, it consists of fixed mark-up, which depends on the aforementioned criteria, and a certain reference indicator, such as LIBOR and EURIBOR. Since all three formulas are very similar and the only difference is in calculating rent rate (i.e., interest rate/profit margin), in the analysis of the acceptability of market rent as the basis for calculating profit margin in Bosnia and Herzegovina which follows, we will only take that difference into account.

Considering the fact that monthly rent is used for calculating the monthly rent rate, it is easy to calculate the annual rent rate the bank charge to the client, which is actually applied profit margin for that financing on an annual level:

$$\%PM\ (g) = \frac{\text{total monthly rent} * 12}{\text{price of the real estate}} * 100$$

Annual profit margin we get based on the monthly rent is especially significant because it allows for comparison with market interest rates of other banks in BIH and profit margins that BBI is currently applying on financings using diminishing musharakah, which are also defined on an annual level. Based on that indicator, it will be easier to make a comparison between the income the bank will generate from its share in real estate in different parts of BIH, if it applies the suggested model of calculating the profit margin based on the market rent, to income it is currently generating from the profit margin based on the credit rating of the client, repayment period, type of collateral, etc.

Let's take the example of a client who is buying a newly built 50 m^2 apartment in Sarajevo at the price of BAM 100,000, and his initial down payment is BAM 10,000 (10%). The client addresses the bank for financing based on diminishing musharakah for the BAM 90,000 he needs to collect the full price. The current monthly rent for a non-furnished apartment of the same size in the same location is estimated at BAM 500 a month. The client has agreed with the bank to gradually pay off the bank's share in partnership over a period of 120 months, after which he will be the only owner of the apartment.

Let's first calculate the annual profit margin which will be applied to this partnership if the monthly rent shared by the partners is BAM 500:

Therefore, the applied profit margin is 6% on an annual level.

$$\%PM = \frac{\text{total monthly rent} * 12}{\text{price of the real estate}} * 100 = \frac{500 * 12}{100,000} * 100$$
$$= \frac{6,000}{100,000} * 100 = 6.00\%$$

In order to calculate the amount that the client will have to pay to the bank during the 120 months, which contains the rent for the bank's share and repayment with the aim for the client to completely pay off the bank's share in ownership by the end of this period, we must first calculate the rent rate x:

$$x = \frac{\text{monthly rent}}{\text{price of the real estate}} = \frac{500}{100,000} = 0.005$$

Now we can calculate the monthly payments, using the annuity formula:

$$M = \frac{x(1+x)^n B_0}{(1+x)^n - 1} = \frac{0.005 * (1+0.005)^{120} * 90,000}{(1+0.005)^{120} - 1}$$
$$= \frac{0.005 * 1.8194 * 90,000}{1.8194 - 1} = \frac{818.73}{0.8194} = 999.18 \text{ KM}$$

Therefore, the monthly payment will be 999.18 BAM.

For the same amount of financing and the same payment period, the client would pay the same amount to BBI, at the profit margin of 6% a year, or to a conventional bank at the interest rate of 6% a year:

$$M = \frac{p(1+p)^n B_0}{(1+p)^n - 1} = \frac{0.005(1+0.005)^{120} * 90,000}{(1+0.005)^{120} - 1} = 999.18 \text{ KM}$$

That is:

$$P = \frac{i(1+i)^n PV}{(1+i)^n - 1} = \frac{0.005(1+0.005)^{120} * 90,000}{(1+0.005)^{120} - 1} = 999.18 \text{ KM}$$

So, the profit BBI could make from its share in partnership in the ownership of a real estate valued at BAM 100,000 and which can be rented in the market at the price of BAM 500 is equal to the revenue that BBI earns using the existing model of calculating the profit margin on financings based on diminishing musharakah with fixed profit margin of 6%, for the same amount of client's down payment and financing, regardless of the period of partnership, and it is also equal to the profit a conventional bank makes on a home loan at an interest rate of 6% a year, for annuity payments.

In the following section, we will make an analysis of the profitability of the suggested model in relation to the existing one, used in BBI currently, taking into consideration several factors which are crucial from the bank's point of view.

5 Analysis of Current Market Rents, Profit Margins in BBI and Interest Rates in the Federation of Bosnia and Herzegovina

There are no limitations for BBI to use rent rate for its financings, according to the laws in Bosnia and Herzegovina, since it is expressed as percentage, like interest rate on loans. Use of variable profit margin, i.e., rent rate, linked to rent index or house pricing index is also allowed by local legislation: The Law on Protection of Financials Services Users of F BiH and The Law on Banks of The Republic of Srpska. However, it could only be applicable for few cities in Bosnia and Herzegovina, since the only official data on real estate price trends are published by the Central Bank of Bosnia and Herzegovina through a yearly real estate price trend index, but only for four cities in The Federation of BIH (FBIH): Sarajevo, Zenica, Mostar and Tuzla in its *Report on Financial Stability.* This index does not include prices for newly built real estate. Federal Statistics Institute publishes the prices of sold apartments in newly built apartment blocks and consumer price indices for Federation of BIH every month, among which they also include the rent index for apartments in the center of the city or the suburbs, for Sarajevo, Zenica, Tuzla, Mostar and Bihać, without making the distinction between old and newly built apartments. Current data available from the Federal Statistics Institute and the Central Bank are, therefore, not completely representative to be sued as an adequate basis for calculating the profit margin for financings based on diminishing musharakah at BBI, since they only offer data on certain types of real estate in a few of the biggest cities in BIH, without offering information on possible deviations in case of differences in age, floor, type and location of the real estate (whether it is in the center of the city or in the outskirts, or in a rural area). Until data and indices for all cities are available, BBI could use those available for the whole country, applying the index and data for the closest city. Fortunately, since these are the biggest cities in BIH with the highest concentration of population, data for most of the properties would be available.

Since we have explained how profit margin would be calculated, let's compare the trends in rents in five of the biggest cities in Federation of BIH for the period between August 2016 and July 2017 and rent rates calculated using the aforementioned formulas, with the trends in market interest rates (which also include applied profit margins at BBI for this period) and profit margins for home financings of natural persons in

BIH. Table 1 lists data about average variations in market rents for the five biggest cities in Federation of BIH, for a 60 m^2, one-bedroom apartment in an apartment block, and data about average market rents and prices of apartments per square meter in Federation of BIH (Edisa Mušanović, e-mail communication, 30 October 2017). Data regarding average prices of sold, newly built apartments for Sarajevo and other municipalities, published by Federal Statistics Institute in a statement entitled *Prices of sold newly-built apartments, II trimester of 2017* were used for calculating the value of a real estate. According to the data in this statement for the second trimester of 2017, the average price of sold, newly built apartments, according to initial information, was BAM 1,705.90, and that calculation was based on 212 apartments sold in Sarajevo and other municipalities. Since the price of the rent was calculated for an apartment of 60 m^2, based on the average cost of a m^2, we calculated the average price of a 60 m^2 apartment in Federation of BIH to be BAM 102,354, and we then used this data to calculate the annual rent rate (the quotient of monthly rent is divided by the price of the real estate and multiplied by twelve months and the number 100—Table 1) (Adapted from the Federal Statistics Agency 2017).

Before we analyze the results in Table 1, we must point to the limitations of the data acquired, in order to get a more precise evaluation of the potential effects. Firstly, the given rent rate does not take into account rents in small towns and villages, since rent rates were calculated based on average rents in central and suburban areas of the largest cities in Federation of BIH. However, since the prices of real estate in small cities and villages are also lower than those in large cities, and since they too would have an impact on the average rent rate, we believe that including those rents in the calculation of average rent rate for FBIH would have no significant impact on the result, although this would depend on the ratio between rents and real estate prices. Furthermore, for calculating the rent rate, we used the price of a square meter in a newly built apartment and these prices are higher than prices for previously owned real estate, whereas the rents apply to both newly build apartment and those that are currently being built. If we took into consideration the average price of both used and newly built apartments, this would result in a somewhat higher rent rate than the one we have here, since the average rent would be divided by a lower average price. Still, that rent rate would not be significantly higher enough to get close to current market interest rates. Also, when calculating the average rent rate for FBIH, all of

Table 1 Comparison of annual rent rate in the largest cities in FBIH for the period between August 2016 and July 2017 with market interest rates and profit margins of BBI for home financings (Adapted from the Federal Statistics Agency 2017)

Year	*Month*	*Bihać*	*Mostar*	*Sarajevo*	*Tuzla*	*Zenica*	*FBIH*	*Annual rent rate (%)*[a]	*Market interest rate (%)*[b]	*Profit margin at BBI (%)*[c]
2016	August	225.00	325.00	325.00	200.00	225.00	260.00	3.048	5.612	5.47
2016	September	225.00	325.00	325.00	200.00	225.00	260.00	3.048	5.628	5.47
2016	October	225.00	325.00	400.00	200.00	225.00	275.00	3.224	5.595	5.59
2016	November	225.00	325.00	400.00	200.00	225.00	275.00	3.224	5.270	5.59
2016	December	225.00	325.00	400.00	200.00	225.00	275.00	3.224	5.277	5.59
2017	January	225.00	325.00	400.00	200.00	225.00	275.00	3.224	5.400	5.59
2017	February	225.00	325.00	400.00	200.00	225.00	275.00	3.224	5.176	4.59
2017	March	225.00	325.00	400.00	250.00	225.00	285.00	3.341	4.922	4.59
2017	April	225.00	325.00	400.00	250.00	225.00	285.00	3.341	4.577	4.59
2017	May	225.00	325.00	400.00	250.00	225.00	285.00	3.341	4.780	4.59
2017	June	225.00	325.00	400.00	250.00	225.00	285.00	3.341	4.869	4.59
2017	July	225.00	325.00	400.00	250.00	225.00	285.00	3.341	4.588	4.59
	Average	225.00	325.00	387.50	220.83	225.00	276.66	3.243	5.14	5.07

[a]Rent rate was calculated based on average prices of rents in FBIH for the period between August 2016 and July 2017 (Edisa Mušanović, e-mail communication, 30 October 2017)

[b]Market interest rates are interest rates for home loans/financings for natural persons with repayment period of over 10 years (including BBI profit margins) (Central Bank of BIH July 2017)

[c]Average profit margins for home financings at BBI with a mortgage as a collateral, repayment period of over 10 years, for clients in the first group (clients working for public institutions and companies and premium LTD and PLC companies) (Bosna Bank International 2016a, b, 2017a, b)

the five biggest cities in FBIH have an equal share, 20%. For a more precise analysis, it would be necessary to apply weighting factors calculated based on the number of home financings sold in each city in relation to the total number of financing sold in these cities. Finally, BBI profit margins used were those for financing the highest level of clients—those who work for government institutions and premium companies for financings for a period of over ten years which have a mortgage as a collateral, and these profit margins are the lowest ones available. A more precise analysis would require including margins for other clients, shorter repayment periods, and other kinds of collateral, which have a significant share in BBI's home financing portfolio. In that case, the discrepancy between average rent rates and average profit margin used would be even more prominent. However, regardless of all these facts, we believe that the variance in the data is acceptable and that it has no significant influence on final conclusions since, according to existing trends, rent rate and market interest rate are significantly different.

As we can see in Table 1, annual rent rate for the period given, which is actually potential annual profit margin that could be applied to FBIH market for financings based on diminishing partnership, if the basis used for profit margin calculation is exclusively the value of market rent, would be 3.243%. This is significantly lower than the average interest rate for long-term home loans which, for this given 12-month period, was 5.14%, and the profit margin for home financings in BBI, which was 5.07%. Therefore, using the existing profit margin creation model, BBI can generate a significantly larger revenue from home financings than it could use a model based on the value of market rent for the given financing volumes.

However, in order to make a valid judgment regarding the influence of the new model on the profitability of the bank, it is necessary to analyze another two factors: competition and expenses. It is evident that, by moving to the suggested model, BBI would significantly decrease its profit margins for home financings which would, on the other hand, lead to a significant increase in the number of financings sold and have a positive impact on profitability. Of course, this begs the question of whether the increase in number of financings sold would be enough to make up for the decrease in profit margins. It is not easy to give an answer to that question, but it is very likely that in the short term it would, because price is virtually the only factor potential clients take into consideration when choosing a bank for their loan/financing, and because other banks would most likely not follow such a drastic decrease in rates immediately. In the long term, however, this is questionable. Credit activity in the BiH market has been stagnating for years and this has led to banks continually decreasing their interest rates in an attempt to attract the clients of other banks. A decrease in interest rates is also evident in the data on market interest rates presented in Table 1.

On the other hand, there is also the issue of whether BBI is able to offer home financings at rates that are equal to current rent rates without jeopardizing its profitability in the long term. It is, of course, impossible to give a single answer to this question, because the funds the bank uses for home financings come from multiple sources. To better illustrate this issue, we can use the information about the profit rates, i.e., interest rates on deposits, as a significant source of revenue for the bank. According to information available in the *Monthly Review of the Central Bank of Bosnia and Herzegovina for July 2017*, interest rates for fixed-term deposits in local currency with a currency clause with a maturity date of over two years for natural persons were 1.512%, and for deposits of non-financial companies 1.795% (Central Bank of BIH July 2017). Taking into consideration, the data on average market rent rate from Table 1 as well, which was 3.341% in July 2017, and with the assumption that the bank finances a majority of home loans from local sources, we can conclude that, according to current market conditions, the use of market rent as the sole basis for calculating the profit margin on financings based on diminishing musharakah is not very viable from the perspective of profitability of home financings in BIH. Here it is also necessary to take into account the costs of credit loss provisions, given the fact that, according to International Accounting Standards and International Financial Reporting Standards, due to exposure to credit risk, the bank is obliged to keep aside a certain percentage of the financing, depending on the level of collateralization, categorization based on the degree of collection and other factors, which decreases the financial results. For a more precise analysis of how acceptable the suggested model of profit margin creation is, it is necessary to take many more factors into account, such as the structure and costs of the sources of funds the bank uses to finance home financings, other costs the bank has and their distribution, clients structure, and personal financings share in total financings.

There is also question of how the application of this type of profit margin calculation would eventually influence the profitability of an Islamic bank in relation to conventional banks and whether this model enables long-term sustainability of Islamic banks. Tahir (2013) mentions that the value of the rent, that could sometimes be so low that the partnership is not profitable for the bank at all could be a problem if we use market rent as a basis for profit that parties in partnership would gain. This is especially the case when the bank finances acquisition of real estates in rural areas or in peripheral areas of small towns, acquisition of old, devastated houses, etc. The application of this model in a market such as Bosnian is definitely not as easy as it may seem at first. Bearing in mind that banks offer the best terms to clients who are financially stable, who earn a lot of money and work in highly profitable companies in an attempt to attract more of those clients, whereas, due to their risk profile, they offer less desirable terms to clients who are not so financially stable, who have fixed-term contracts at their companies, or who work in companies which are less profitable, we must ask what effects the application of calculating the profit margin based on market rent would have on the profitability of an Islamic bank. A possible scenario in the case of calculating the profit margin based on market rent is that, due to high profit margins on their luxury real estate, premium clients would choose a more affordable offer of a conventional bank, whereas poorer clients, those who have less stable and lower income, would choose the offer of the Islamic bank, which would be more affordable for them, based on the characteristics of the real estate that they are buying. This could lead to a major change in the structure of the clients of the Islamic bank, and the loss of premium clients and an increase in the number of poorer clients, which could, in the long term, have a significant impact on the profitability and stability of the Islamic bank, due to the profile of these clients. How pronounced this impact would be would depend on several factors, including the ratio between rent and real estate price, the ratio between rent and interest rate/profit margin, as well as purchasing power of the population (which is not very high in BIH and could thus have a significant impact, considering the fact that in such conditions, price elasticity of demand is higher).

Still, we believe that for the purposes of this paper, the given analysis is enough to conclude that, in the current conditions in the market regarding rent rates, costs of sources and interest rates of competitors for home loans, the application of calculating profit margins based on market rents is currently not profitable for home financings in the long term.

6 Combination of the Two Models—The Best Solution in Current Market Conditions

Considering the aforementioned problems with using the rent as a basis for calculating the profit margin for financings based on diminishing musharakah at BBI Sarajevo, and its advantages as a realistic basis for partnerships in ownership of real estates, we believe that in the current market conditions it cannot be accepted as the only basis for calculating the profit margin, but that it should not be completely disregarded as such. Taking into consideration all the arguments for and against its application, we believe that the optimal model is actually a combination of these two models—the one currently being applied by BBI, with certain changes, and the model based exclusively on the market rent value. Since it is obvious that the application of the market rent as the only basis for determining the prices of financing in the existing conditions jeopardizes short-term profitability, due to extremely low values of rents and ratio between rent and market real estate prices, and especially long-term profitability of the bank, due to the tendency of financially stable and highly ranked clients to leave and attracting more risky categories of clients, those with low and unstable income and low credit rating, we suggest a model that would, in addition to market rent, take client risk profile as the basis for calculating the profit margin. In the model that we suggest, the first factor which will determine the profit margin for financings based on diminishing musharakah would be market rent. Market rent and real estate prices would be determined using available statistical data and, for those areas where statistical data is not available, based on special methodology of estimating the market value of rent and the value of real estate, which the client will learn about when they sign the financing contract. The second factor would depend on the estimate of client's ability to pay off the financing in the future and will be calculated as a percentage value which will be given to different client categories, depending on their risk profile. This factor will be lower for less risky categories—clients with high income, who work for stable companies with permanent employment status, and higher for categories estimated by the bank to be more risky, such as clients who work for companies which are experiencing financial losses, clients with low income, and clients who are already indebted.

According to the suggested model, the annual profit margin which would be applied to financings based on the model of diminishing musharakah and ijarah would be calculated using the following formula:

$$\%\text{PM} = x + r_f = \left(\frac{\text{total monthly rent}}{\text{price of the real estate}} * 12 * 100\right) + r_f$$

where r_f is the risk factor of the client and financing calculated as a certain percentage, based on the bank's estimates.

According to that, monthly payments, taking into account the new factor, would be calculated using this formula:

$$M = \frac{p_1(1 + p_1)^n B_0}{(1 + p_1)^n - 1}$$

where p_1 is the new monthly rate calculated using the following formula:

$$p_1 = \frac{\text{total monthly rent}}{\text{price of the real estate}} + \frac{r_f}{12 * 100}$$

The aim of applying the risk factor is to minimize the aforementioned drawbacks of using market rent as the only base for calculating the profit margin. The risk factor will actually increase the price of the financing in order to ensure bank's profitability, and it will depend on:

(a) the risks the bank is exposed to when entering the partnership, based on the profile of individual client and the collateral,
(b) market interest rates applied by other banks to loans with similar purposes and repayment,
(c) opportunity costs of investment in other forms of partnership and other projects,
(d) expected return on capital expected by the shareholders from the bank, taking into account projected revenue from all the bank's activities, costs of sources and other costs,
(e) obligatory provisions for credit losses.

The purpose of increasing the rate for all client categories is to achieve the primary goal and main condition for long-term sustainability of the bank—profit. The purpose of differentiating the profit margins for different client categories is to reduce premium client attrition and to increase the number of premium clients, with acceptable, but not so low profit margins for clients with lower, less stable income as to result in a significant increase in the number of clients with bad credit rating from other banks.

7 Conclusion

Although it may seem at first that the model suggested has not offered a significant improvement to the existing model at BBI, we believe it is the optimal solution for current market conditions. Despite the fact that the model of calculating the profit margin based on the market value of rent may ensure just treatment of poorer clients and although rent is the only realistic basis for financings based on partnership in real estate ownership, it is still not possible to ignore profitability and stability of the bank as the long-term goals of shareholders, depositors, and regulatory agencies. Of course, conditions in the market—rent values and prices of real estate, as well as offers of other banks—have to be monitored constantly. When the conditions change, the bank would also change the risk factors for each client category, and, in case of more prominent changes, the structure of the profit margin as well.

However, regardless of the aforementioned drawbacks, we believe that the suggested model of calculating the profit margin is justified and is a good solution, considering the financing model, existing legal issues and Shariah laws. Final judgment on this issue can, however, only be given after the suggested model is practically applied, when all the advantages and drawbacks could be analyzed and compared with the ones of the existing model.

Considering the trend of decreasing interest rates and profit margins for loans and an increase in market rents, accompanied by a decrease in interest rates and profit rates for deposits in BiH, it is expected that rent and interest rates/profit margins will get even closer to one another in the near future. This trend will have a positive impact on credit activity in Bosnia and Herzegovina market, since, in the long term, buying an apartment will become increasingly more profitable than renting one. It is also expected that statistics agencies in BiH will, in the meantime, start publishing data on trends in real estate prices and appropriate indices, which will enable Islamic banks to use these indices to adjust their profit margins for long-term financings, if the Shariah boards approve it. In that case, the basic model for calculating the profit margin based on trends in rents and real estate prices, without the suggested corrections, will be more acceptable for Islamic banks in BIH. Last but not least, full application of this model and estimate of its effectiveness are possible only if the expected changes in regulations in Southeast Europe countries, including Bosnia and Herzegovina take place, enabling Islamic banks to operate in their full capacities. That would definitely attract investors from Islamic countries and lead to expansion of Islamic banking, contributing to further development and growth of financial markets and economies of Southeast Europe.

References

Journal Articles

Meera, A. K. M., and Abdul Razak, D. 2009. Home Financing Through the musharakah mutanaqisah Contracts: Some Practical Issues. *Journal of King Abdulaziz University, Islamic Economy*, 22 (1): 3–27. http://www.kau.edu.sa/Files/320/Researches/54963_25288.pdf.

Tahir, S. 2013. Alternative Structures for Financing by Islamic Banks. IRTI Working Paper 1434 (3): 98–106.

Books

Usmani, T. U. 2003. Uvod u islamske finansije (An Introduction to Islamic Finance). Translated by Ahmet Alibašić and Amel Kovačević. Živinice, Bosna i Hercegovina: Selsebil.

Conference Proceedings

Rama, A., Wardhana, W., Rahman, F. K., and Ferdian, I. R. n.d. Islamic Benchmarking: An Alternative to Interest Rate (Evidence from Home Financing in Malaysia). *Paper Presented at 4th CBA International Conference 2010 Global Economic Direction*. Available on http://www.cba.edu.kw/wtou/download/conf4/Ali.pdf. Accessed July 2016.

Statistics/Datasets

Centralna banka Bosne i Hercegovine (The Central Bank of BIH). (2017, July). *Mjesečni ekonomski pregled, juli 2017 (Monthly Economic Review, July 2017)*. Available from http://www.cbbh.ba/content/DownloadAttachment/?id=8228ac52-6e67-45d8-8927-605bfe6ab7e7&langTag=bs.

Federalni zavod za statistiku (Federal Statistics Institute). *Cijene prodatih novih stanova, II tromjesečje 2017 (Prices of Sold Newly-Built Apartments, II Trimester of 2017)*, p. 2. August 21, 2017. Available from http://www.fzs.ba/index.php/2017/08/21/cijene-prodatih-novi-stanova-ii-tromjesecje-2017/prvi-rezultati/.

Corporate Documents

Bosna Bank International. 2015. Odluka o profitnim maržama za finansiranja i stopama prinosa na depozite BBI dd Sarajevo (Decision on Profit margins for Financings and Profit Rates on Deposits of BBI Sarajevo).

Bosna Bank International. 2016a. Akcija Tarifa i uslovi finansiranja BBI – fizička lica, Verzija 1.1 (Tariff and Conditions of Financings for Natural Persons, Version 1.1).

Bosna Bank International. 2016b. Tarifa i uslovi finansiranja BBI – fizička lica, Verzija 1.2 (Tariff and Conditions of Financings for Natural Persons, Version 1.2).

Bosna Bank International. 2017a. Akcija finansiranja BBI – fizička lica, Verzija 1.0 (Tariff of BBI Financings for Natural Persons, Version 1.0).

Bosna Bank International. 2017b. Akcija Tarifa i uslovi finansiranja BBI – fizička lica, Verzija 1.1 (Tariff of BBI Financings for Natural Persons, Version 1.1).

Bosna Bank International. 2017c. Pravilnik o profitnim maržama za finansiranje i stopama prinosa na depozite BBI dd Sarajevo (Rulebook on Profit Margins for Financings and Profit Rates on Deposits of BBI Sarajevo).

Index

V. Efendic (ed.), *Islamic Finance Practices*, https://doi.org/10.1007/978-3-030-34420-7

The manufacturer's authorised representative in the EU is Springer Nature Customer Service Centre GmbH, Europaplatz 3, 69115 Heidelberg, Germany. If you have any concerns regarding our products, please contact ProductSafety@springernature.com

Printed and bound by CPI Group (UK) Ltd, Croydon, CR0 4YY
06/10/2026
02228561-0001